SUICIDE AND THE SOUL

DUNQUIN SERIES

Rare monographs and translations, symbolism, and depth psychology. (A peninsula pointing across the Atlantic toward America, Dunquin lies at the farthest fringe of European civilization.)

SUICIDE
AND THE SOUL

by

JAMES HILLMAN

Spring Publications, Inc.
Dallas, Texas

This edition has been photo-offprinted from the typography of the
1973 Harper Colophon edition (Standard Book Number 06-090329-5)
with kind permission. Original hardcover editions were published in
London (1964) by Hodder and Stoughton and in New York (1964) by
Harper & Row. Translations into German, Swedish, Italian, Danish, and
Japanese have been printed.

Published by Spring Publications, Inc.; P.O. Box 222069;
Dallas, Texas 75222
Printed in the United States of America

International Distributors:
Spring; Postfach; 8803 Ruschlikon; Switzerland.
Japan Spring Sha, Inc.; 12-10, 2-Chome,
Nigawa Takamaru; Takarazuka 665, Japan.
Element Books Ltd; Longmead Shaftesbury;
Dorset SP7 8PL; England.
Astam Books Pty. Ltd.; 27B Llewellyn St.;
Balmain, Sydney, N.S.W. 2041; Australia.

Library of Congress Cataloging in Publication Data
Hillman, James.
Suicide and the soul.

Reprint. Originally published: New York : Harper
& Row, 1973.
1. Suicide.   2. Death.   3. Psychoanalysis.
I. Title.
RC569.H54   1985   616.85'8445   85-11901
ISBN 0-88214-208-9

TO
ESTHER STRAUS

Acknowledgments

The lines from "Healing" by D. H. Lawrence from *Selected Poems* are reproduced on p. 96 by permission of The Viking Press, copyright 1916 by D. H. Lawrence, 1920 by B. W. Huebsch, Inc., 1929 by Jonathan Cape and Harrison Smith, Inc., 1944 by Frieda Lawrence.

The lines from "East Coker" from *Four Quartets* by T. S. Eliot are reproduced on p. 155 by permission of Harcourt, Brace & World, Inc.

CONTENTS

Prefatory Note

Part One
SUICIDE AND ANALYSIS

Part Two
THE CHALLENGE OF ANALYSIS

PREFATORY NOTE

(1964)

GOING into questions of death and suicide means breaking open taboos. Opening issues that have long been encrusted requires force, and the harder the defences, the more one has to press one's point. So this little book shows argument. It questions suicide prevention; it examines the death experience; it approaches the suicide problem not from the viewpoints of life, society, and 'mental health', but in relation to death and the soul. It regards suicide not only as an exit from life but also as an entrance to death. To turn matters about in this way disrupts official attitudes, especially those of medicine. So medicine will be provoked and 'lay analysis' supported from a fresh perspective of psychology. This wholly other view arises from the enquiry into suicide as it is experienced through the vision of death in the soul.

Whatever one says about the human soul—if it hits its mark at all—will be both right and wrong. Psychological material is so complex that every statement is inadequate. We can no more stand back from the psyche and look at it objectively than we can get away from ourselves. If we are anything we are psyche. And, because the unconscious makes relative every formulation of consciousness by complementing it with an opposite and equally valid position, no psychological statement can have certainty. The truth remains uncertain, since death the only certainty does not reveal its truth. Human frailty nowhere sets more the limits to a work than in psychology. The choice then becomes: stop speaking in wisdom or speak out anyway in consciousness of folly. This book is a product of the second course.

PREFATORY NOTE
(1976)

ANOTHER printing offers the chance to say more. For instance, more needs to be said about the shadowy aspects of suicide: aggression, revenge, blackmail, sado-masochism, body-hatred. Suicidal moves give us a clue about our 'inner-killer,' who this shadow is, and what it wants. Since suicide moves show this shadow using the body as an instrument for concrete aims (revenge, hatred, etc.), profound questions are raised about relations between suicide attempts and attempts at literalizing reality by means of the body.

So more could be said about the literalism of suicide—for the danger lies not in the death fantasy but in its literalism. So suicidal literalism might be reversed to mean: literalism is suicidal. Although the feeling of death as metaphor, and the view of suicide as an attempt toward this metaphor, permeates the whole book, more needs to be said about the archetypal background of this perspective toward death. Since 1964 I have been working on just that, and I invite the reader who would inquire still further into matters broached in this book to look at my several writings on the senex archetype, on pathologizing, literalism and metaphor in *Re-Visioning Psychology*, and also at the 1973 and 1974 Eranos lectures, "The Dream and the Underworld" and "On the Necessity of Abnormal Psychology." This book presaged those later essays on human darkness.

As before, I wish to thank the persons who contributed to this book in one way or another: the anonymous ones with whom I worked in practice, and those mentioned in the first edition—Eleanor Mattern, Adolf Guggenbühl, Carlos Drake, Robin Denniston, A. K. Donoghue, Elisabeth Peppler, David Cox, Marvin Spiegelman, John Mattern, and Catharina Hillman.

Part One

SUICIDE AND ANALYSIS

"Things naturall to the Species, are not always so for the individuall."
(John Donne: *Biathanatos*: A declaration of that
Paradoxe or thesis, that Selfe-homicide is not so
Naturally Sinne, that it may never be otherwise, 1644)

"There is but one truly serious philosophical problem and that is suicide.
Judging whether life is or is not worth living amounts to answering the
fundamental question of philosophy. All the rest . . . comes afterwards.
These are games; one must first answer."
(Albert Camus: *The Myth of Sisyphus*, 1942)

"Despite appearances to the contrary, the establishment of order and the
dissolution of what has been established are at bottom beyond human control. The secret is that only that which can destroy itself is truly alive."
(C. G. Jung: *Psychology and Alchemy*, 1944)

"Is it not for us to confess that in our civilized attitude towards death we
are once more living psychologically beyond our means, and must reform
and give truth its due? Would it not be better to give death the place in
actuality and in our thoughts which properly belongs to it, and to yield a
little more prominence to that unconscious attitude towards death which
we have hitherto so carefully suppressed? . . . *Si vis vitam, para mortem.*
If you would endure life, be prepared for death."
(Sigmund Freud: *Thoughts on War and Death*, 1915)

"Oh build your ship of death, oh build it in time
and build it lovingly, and put it between the hands of
your soul."
(D. H. Lawrence: *Ship of Death*, MS.'B'.)

CHAPTER I

THE PROBLEM

ANY careful consideration of life entails reflections of death, and the confrontation with reality means facing mortality. We never come fully to grips with life until we are willing to wrestle with death. We need not postulate a death drive nor need we speculate about death and its place in the scheme of things to make a simple point: every deep and complex concern, whether in oneself or with another, has in it the problem of death. And the problem of death is posed most vividly in suicide. Nowhere else is death so near. If we want to move towards self-knowledge and the experience of reality, then an enquiry into suicide becomes the first step.

Because analysis is just such a careful consideration of life it is occupied with questions of death. It provides the intense human situation for focusing essential questions, thereby becoming a paradigm of life. Everything is bared within a small room, between two people, in secrecy and vacuum. Sinister topics belong because analysis is an activity more of the left hand than of the right. It is concerned with taboos and set within a taboo of its own. The goal of adaptation to the social order is of the right hand, of conscious counselling. But analysis includes the left as well. It reveals the inferior man where he is awkward and sinister, and where suicide is a real matter. Analysis gives to the left hand an opportunity to live consciously its own life without the right hand sitting in judgment knowing what it is doing. The right hand can never know the left hand, only interpret and transpose.

Therefore by taking up the question of suicide through

analysis we have a possibility not given by statistics, case studies, or the research literature—all methods invented by the right hand. Because analysis is life in microcosm, especially the dark side, what is found there is widely applicable in other close personal involvements where reason is not enough. The discoveries can be transposed to the suicide problem as it may arise elsewhere in life.

And it is *in life* that suicide arises. Contrary to popular imaginings, suicide is more likely to occur in the home than in the asylum. It happens to the famous of whom we read, or next door to someone we know, or in the family—or in oneself. Like any turn of fortune—love, tragedy, glory—suicide is matter for the psychiatrist only when it is distorted, only when it forms part of a psychotic syndrome. In itself, suicide is neither syndrome nor symptom. Therefore this enquiry may not be specialised; it will instead take up suicide in the human setting of analysis, that is, as it could and does appear within the normal course of any life.

Suicide is the most alarming problem of life. How can one be prepared for it? How can one understand it? Why does one do it? Why does one not? It seems irrevocably destructive, leaving behind guilt and shame and hopeless amazement. So too in analysis. For the analyst it is even more complex than psychosis, sexual temptation, or physical violence, because suicide represents the epitome of the responsibility an analyst carries. Moreover, it is fundamentally insoluble because it is not a problem of life, but of life and death, bringing with it all of death's imponderables. The consideration of suicide also brings consideration of the ultimates. By discovering his stand towards this problem, an analyst will also be forming his attitude towards first or last things, turning and shaping the vessel of his calling.

An analyst's opinions about religion, about education,

about politics, adultery and divorce, even about holidays, drinking, smoking, and diet, ought not to interfere in his analytical work. During his training he considers his own beliefs, habits, and ethics so that they do not present obstacles to the other person. Because a personal point of view only is not adequate for meeting the problems of the analytic hour, training aims at increasing objectivity. When suicide is the problem of the hour an analyst should be expected to have achieved a conscious point of view beyond his subjective concerns. But how does an analyst develop objectivity about suicide?

Objectivity means openness; and openness about suicide is not easily gained. The law has found it criminal, religion calls it a sin, and society turns away from it. It has been long the habit to hush it up or excuse it by insanity, as if it were the primary anti-social aberration. Objectivity here puts one immediately outside the collective. Openness to suicide means more than taking an individual stand against collective moral opinion. *An objective enquiry in this field somehow betrays the impulse of life itself.* The question raised in this enquiry necessarily leads beyond the touch of life. But only death is beyond the touch of life, so that openness to suicide means first of all a movement towards death, openly and without dread.

It is a practical matter. A new person arrives and you notice marks on the wrist. During early interviews it comes out that there were two suicide attempts some years ago, secretive and almost successful. The person wants to work only with you because a friend had referred her to you and she cannot bring herself to trust anyone else. By accepting this person you accept the threat that at the next crisis she may again attempt suicide, yet it is your work to maintain an analytical tension which does not shy away from crises.

Another has cancer and is in increasingly severe pain.

For family and financial reasons he judges he should die now rather than suffer through—and drive his family to suffer, too—the last stages of his medically predicted time. Nor does he want to die drugged stuporous against pain and cheated of experiencing death. From his state of mind, his dreams, and his religious convictions he is certain there is a time to die and that it has come. He has achieved a philosophical point of view and does not want to exhaust his strength in argument. He seeks your sympathy and guidance during this final step.

A young man barely misses death in a car accident. He dreams that he is living in the suicide problem, but that he must not yet look at it because he is still not strong enough to handle it. He worries because he cannot feel the impact of the dream, yet knows somewhere that he is in danger. He wants to work it out with you. If you follow the dream and do not look at the problem with him he may again have an accident, a suicide substitute. If you follow his concern and go into the suicide problem with him he may not be able to manage it, and the dream might come 'true'.

A fourth person receives uncanny messages from an idolised dead parent who committed suicide in keeping with a peculiar family tradition. He feels there is a compelling reason in answering the ancestral call; death grows in fascination. Besides, the dreams show lamed or dying figures indicating a psychological content which, as it enters consciousness, may paralyse the impulse to live, fulfilling the nemesis.

The lay analyst—as non-medical analysts are generally called—is all alone facing these decisions: he has no prepared position or social organisation to help him meet the dangers. He has a unique relationship to the other person, a relationship which implies closer responsibility for the other's destiny in this moment than has a husband for a wife, a son for a parent, or brothers for each other, mainly because he is privy in a special way to the other's mind and heart. Not only does he know what others do not know, but the analytical situation itself places him in the role of an arbiter of fate. This unique relationship together with all its complicated expectations about their joint destiny has been called the transference. Through it an analyst is involved in the other's life as no one else is. The transference is a league of the two through thick and thin and, at times, against all others. This private league is fundamental to analysis. It is similar to the relationship of lawyer to client, physician to patient, confessor to penitent. In other vocations, however, this bond of trust is an accessory to the work, important, but—as we shall see farther on—having to be waived in those exigencies where it conflicts with the fundamental principles of those vocations. But transference is the root of analysis; it can never be set aside for other principles without breaking the therapeutic vessel. It is the living symbol of the healing process and expresses the continually changing and gripping eros of analysis.

Because transference is so complicated, so emotional, and so mysterious, it has resisted explanations. The term itself is used differently by different analysts. It can perhaps be better understood by comparing it with the model of secrecy, silence, and 'against all others' which is operative in other profound works of the soul—creation of art, religious mysteries, passionate love. Participants in the unique relationship of analysis share a common mystery as do lovers, explorers, initiants, who have together been touched by the same experience. The participants in this *via sinistra* are accomplices; the suicide of one means nothing less than the complicity of the other.

For the psychiatrist the situation is different. He has been trained medically, and we shall take time to look into the effects of this training as we go along. Here we can say this much: the psychiatrist has a prepared position from which to meet the threat of suicide. He is not alone in the same way as is the analyst because he is not open in the same way. His view of transference has other grounds which lead him to participate in the healing process differently. Above all, he knows beforehand what his task is regarding suicide: to save life. He has means to do this immediately, for example, through physical methods of treatment (shock, injections, pills). He has authority, varying from country to country, to commit the patient to an asylum, at least temporarily for prevention of suicide. As with the soldier, the policeman, or the judge, death occurs within the medical man's line of duty. He is not held accountable, except perfunctorily and in unusual cases. He has professional opinion with him should there be a mistake. To the world he is not 'lay'. The backing of the profession and the fact that he is considered the foremost specialist in judging this sort of question give security to his decisions and comfort to his conscience.

Moreover, medical mistakes are part of medical work. There are mistakes in surgery, obstetrics, anaesthetics, mistakes in diagnosis and medication. No one demands that medicine be perfect. In the battle against death the physician is expected to fight unceasingly, but not to win every time. The physician to some degree must become accustomed to the death of his charges, since physical death has been his daily companion from the beginning of his studies in anatomical dissection.

The psychiatrist has less chance of making dramatic mistakes than has the internist or the surgeon. He has less chance of losing a patient through death—except by suicide. Since death is the clearest 'mistake' for the medically trained man, a psychiatrist could tend to regard suicide as a surgeon regards a failed operation.

For an analyst, mistakes are judged from another angle. His first concern is always with *the health of the soul*, and therefore his standards of judgment concern psychological—not physical—life. We shall see as we go along that psychological health does not have to reveal itself in external physical performance; therefore, an analyst's mistakes are more difficult to discover and to assess. The scars and crippling do not show in the same way. The expectations of analytical work are also more complex than those of medicine, and the lines of success and failure in analysis are less clear. Also, because analytical work is a relationship, a relationship requiring the commitment of the analyst's personality, an analyst is always involved in every event. This involvement goes beyond medical responsibility for a charge; it is rather a participation in the other as if it were oneself. Thus the death of his charge is always to the analyst his own death, his own suicide, his own failure. An analyst faced again and again with suicidal people is forced to consider his own death and where he is lacking, because the people who come for therapy bring the analyst his own problems. This attitude differs from that of the physician, who does not regard the diseases and complaints brought to his consulting room as somehow belonging also to him. The unique relationship involving the analyst with the other at the same time prevents anyone else from the same sort of participation in the case, so that an analyst carries each death alone.

His training has not prepared him enough for this. He is confronted with death without having had a privileged access to the dead and dying as the physician has had in his training. An analyst's road to it has been psychological, that is, through the death experience in his own psyche. His training analysis was an initiation into psychological death. An initiation, however, is only a beginning. An analyst remains lay if, in this most crucial area of his work, he does not confront psychological death with that constancy with which the physician meets physical death. By working out his position to suicide an analyst moves towards this confrontation. It helps bring him closer to the death experience, developing his objectivity and giving him a competence to meet it psychologically comparable to the competence of the physician with physical death.

Were the psychiatrist also to be an analyst, we would seem to have the ideal solution: medical analysis. On the one hand, he could work psychologically, entering into the unique relationship with the patient; while on the other, he would have the armoury of medicine from which to draw whenever suicide loomed. This is, in fact, the general pattern today. (Both medical and lay analysts tend to be psychological in approach up to the point of suicide, when they both tend to become medical.) There would hardly be reason to go on with this discussion were it not for this basic question: is not medical analysis, rather than an ideal solution, in fact more problematic than either medicine or analysis alone?

The points of view demanded by medicine and by analysis are hard to combine. Can one practise analysis and yet retain the point of view of modern scientific medicine? Or can one accept consistently the point of view of a depth psychology which affirms the soul and practise orthodox medicine? We shall see in later chapters that soul and body can present conflicting demands. There are times when the claims of life demand that values of the soul be jettisoned. If one stands for life, as must the physician, the psychological considerations must take a secondary place. Examples of this are found in any asylum where, for the protection of life and the prevention of suicide, every sort of violent psychological insult is used to 'normalise' the suffering soul. In fact, every caution, every prescription, every treatment in modern medicine has an anti-psychological component, whether it be in the form of tranquillisers, which are evidently so, or simply in the form of bandaging and splinting, which seem only technical matters. Treatment of the body does not affect the body alone. Something is being done to the psyche, too, which may well be positive, but will surely be negative if the possible effects on the soul are refused or ignored. *Whenever treatment directly neglects the experience as such and hastens to reduce or overcome it, something is being done against the soul.* For experience is the soul's one and only nourishment.

If one stands for psychological life, as the analyst must, physical life may have to be thwarted and left unfulfilled in order to meet the soul's claims, its pressing concerns with redemption. This seems to go against all common sense, all medical practice, and all rational philosophy of *mens sana in corpore sano*. Yet the experiment of life continually throws up examples where the body is only second, and every neurosis shows this priority of psyche over soma.

This tension of body and soul is crystallised most clearly in the problem of suicide. Here, the body can be destroyed by a 'mere fantasy'. No other question forces us so acutely into facing the reality of the psyche as a reality equal to the body. And because all analysis turns on the axis of psychic reality, suicide becomes the paradigmatic experience of all analysis, perhaps of all life.

CHAPTER II

SUICIDE PREVENTION: THE VIEWPOINTS OF SOCIOLOGY, LAW, THEOLOGY AND MEDICINE

An enquiry should properly start in those fields having the most to do with suicide. There one would expect help in forming one's view. However, old arguments for and against suicide and the justification for these arguments must be side-stepped. Interesting as they might be, they do not lead to fresh ground. An analytical enquiry differs from others in that it does not set out to condemn suicide nor condone it, nor even judge it in any way, but simply to understand it as a fact of psychological reality. How do others look at this reality? And more, a psychological enquiry must also ask: why do others look at this reality in this way or that? In order to gain help in shaping one's own attitude one has to investigate what shaped other attitudes. And so the enquiry must begin with the roots of the suicide arguments as psychological attitudes stemming from fundamental models of thinking operative in the fields where suicide is most discussed.

All of us, no matter what the vocation, work from certain root metaphors. These models of thought stand behind and govern the way we view the problems we meet in our professions. These metaphors are not so much carefully worked-out conscious philosophies as they are half-conscious attitudes rooted in the structure of the psyche itself. The study of root metaphors is part of the history of ideas. Owing to Jung's investigations into the archetypal nature of these fundamental patterns of viewing the world, the history of ideas is becoming more empirical and psychological, more relevant to actual life, because these same models of thought operate through the unconscious in the attitudes of everybody.

Root metaphors are not something we can pick up and cast off at will. They are traditional, handed down through the profession itself, so that when we take up a professional task we step into an archetypal role. Where tradition is alive, the archetypal background of it carries those who are related to it. It is more powerful in many respects than the individual, contributing to the effectiveness of the individual's professional efforts.

Consider, for example, the sociologist. The root metaphor which governs his attitudes and to which he gives his loyalty is Society. Society is a living reality for him. It provides a way of understanding himself; it offers a model of thought from which he can deduce hypotheses, and a field of facts where the hypotheses can be tested and applied. New facts will be first related to this model, and the better they can be taken up by it, the more effective the sociologist.

Emile Durkheim, who can be considered the founder of modern sociology, wrote a major work on suicide. It was the first exhaustive study from the sociological point of view, and nowhere can one find the sociologist's account of suicide stated more clearly. From the statistics of suicide, even the crude ones of the last century, a given number of suicides can be expected in a given year, and these can be further predicted for types, age, and sex of suicides. The sociologist knows that next year in the United States there will be at least eighteen thousand suicides, of which a certain proportion will take place in cities, a certain proportion will be of young mothers, a certain proportion will be by drowning, etc.

These figures are so generally reliable that suicide is

an established sociological phenomenon, an independently valid fact, year in and year out, group by group, region by region. It is one of the basic social facts and (therefore, for sociology) cannot be accounted for by studying the individuals this year or next who happen to make up the expected quotient. Suicide is a collective tendency of the social body with its own existence, manifesting itself by taking a certain toll yearly.

By fulfilling certain conditions, an individual becomes suicidal and then makes the attempt. These conditions Durkheim and sociologists since his time have carefully analysed. Anyone can become suicidal whenever he enters these particular social conditions which form a stable variable within each society. Durkheim says: "The causes of death are outside rather than within us, and are effective only if we venture into their sphere of activity" (Durkheim, p. 43).

Because the individual is enmeshed in the suicidal tendency of a group owing to which suicide results, the act as such cannot be moral or immoral. No personal choice is involved. Suicide is rather a sociological problem, telling us something about the condition of a society. For sociology, this condition is always negative. Suicide represents a loosening of the social structure, a weakening of group bonds, a disintegration. It thus attacks the root metaphor of sociology itself. As an open enemy of society, it must be opposed and prevented.

Sociology occupies itself ardently with the prevention problem, and Durkheim made many influential recommendations here. The main aim is to bring the individual back into a group from which he has become estranged through divorce or widowhood, success or failure, etc., for it is the movement towards individual isolation that leads to the suicidal tendency. *Suicide prevention for sociology means group reinforcement, which of course reinforces the root metaphor of sociology itself.* It grows clearer why sociologists are so exercised about suicide. It also becomes evident that it is not suicide which is the fundamental tendency to be prevented, but the *disintegrating influence of individuality*.

If the prevention of suicide merges with the prevention of individuality, an analyst can hardly turn to sociology for his standpoint. He reads movements towards isolation, individuality, and the loosening of bonds with the collective in quite another light.

Turning to the legal point of view towards suicide, we find it declared criminal by three of the great traditions upon which Western justice stands: Roman law, Church law, and English law. In 1809 Blackstone stated in the fifteenth edition of his *Commentaries* that because suicide is against God and King "the law has therefore ranked this among the highest crimes".

Prevention of suicide is again the main end in view. Blackstone suggests one way of counteracting female suicide which would at the same time benefit the study of anatomy. He deems it a "wise law" if the coroner would deliver the dead body to "be mangled by the surgeon's knife, and exposed to public view". John Wesley, the first Methodist reformer, had a similar imaginative bent. In 1790, he too proposed that the naked bodies of female suicides be dragged through the streets. Desecration of the corpse was an antique form of showing how heinous the crime. Until 1870 the deterrent against suicide in English law was mainly against the physical property of the deceased rather than against the physical body. The property of those who committed suicide while of sound mind was declared forfeit to the crown. Until 1961 English law still held that the estate of the deceased could be penalised; life insurance was not paid out to the

27

beneficiary unless previously stipulated. Today, an abettor of the deed, as the survivor of a suicide pact, can be considered in many countries an accessory to a crime. In some states of the United States, attempted suicide is still a criminal act.

As sociology upholds society, law stands for justice. The principles of justice can be derived from three relations: man with God, man with his fellow man, man with himself. The separation of church and state and the secularisation of law has largely removed the first kind of justice from contemporary law. Justice of the second kind concerns the preservation of the social contract. The family, the institutions of the state, the contracts between bodies, the duties and rights of citizens, the ownership of property, all require stability guaranteed by law. The law guarantees this stability by weaving continuity into its fabric, by providing for smooth transitions and future eventualities. Sudden death tears the fabric, which the jurist then stitches together with threads pulled from many places: rights of succession and title, death clauses, wills, inheritance-tax structure, and the like. Provisions for an 'act of God' are written into legal papers, while death is an eventuality foreseen as *'force majeure'*. But such death, albeit sudden, is exogenous. As Durkheim said: "The causes of death are outside rather than within us . . ." The law would seem to take cognisance of only a *deus ex machina* who acts from outside. Death from suicide, because it originates within one's own person, is neither *'force majeure'* nor an 'act of God', but a one-sided abrogation of contract. By wilfully tearing the fabric, it breaks the law.

The third kind of justice—the relation of man with himself—has never been a province of the law proper, except to protect the individual from losing his rights to this relation with himself through encroachments from others.

Guarantees of personal liberty permit man to have internal justice, but they do not describe its nature. Descriptions of how a man should or should not worship, think, speak, have even been considered infringements upon his internal justice. For much of continental law, suicide would seem to belong among the unexpressed rights of man. But for the three great pillars of Western law, suicide was not judged in terms of man's relation to himself. It was judged from the outside, as if man belonged first to God and King and last to himself. Again, we are told man cannot serve both his own individuality and his God and society.

When law does not recognise suicide as a right to be protected, as it protects freedoms and possessions, does it not allow others to infringe upon one's relation with oneself? Are we not then prevented from the outside from following what we may conceive to be our destiny? Are we not being ordered by law to live?

The interference with internal justice in the name of interpersonal or social justice has been severe indeed. The legal tradition in England has held that of all kinds of homicide, suicide alone was without justification or excuse. Suicide (until 1961) has always been considered a felony, an act of murder; whereas self-defence, the execution of public justice, and preventing a felonious act are all forms of justifiable homicide. Misadventure, chance medley, resisting illegal arrest, and protection (as against rape, for instance) are all forms of excusable homicide. In other words, the legal tradition has been: we might kill others in many ways and on many grounds without breaking the law. But we could never in any circumstances justifiably or excusably kill ourselves. The argument says I may not be 'mine own executioner'. In some circumstances I may kill others with the sanction of public justice, but only public justice may permit a citizen to leave its domain.

The law has not set up a tribunal to pass on suicide requests, so there is no way to opt out of the social contract by going to death intentionally except through breaking the law. The man who committed suicide was guilty and could never prove himself innocent. An analyst who accepts the traditional legal point of view can never justify a suicide.

The law left one loophole—insanity. By wiping out the applicability of the second kind of justice, the law made room for the third kind. By finding a man no longer competent to be governed by the rules of the social contract based on reason, his death no longer tears the fabric. He is no longer woven into the legal structure; his word and deed are outside the frame. To the rational society, he has in a sense already died.

This means at its worst that justice is performed by defamation of character. To be saved from being found a murderer, one was defined a lunatic. The phrase was: "whilst the balance of his mind was disturbed". The 'sane' suicide was consequently hushed up or disguised as an accident.

Is this also the analyst's way out? Hardly, since his task is to find the sanity and understand the reason in the acts of each individual. To concur in this legal opinion would be to enmesh all the differences and to declare as madness every suicide, no matter how each appears from within.

In searching for the root metaphor which supports the suicide injunctions and suicide prevention by law and society, we must turn to the Bible. Religious law precedes secular law, and the commandment "Thou shalt not kill" provides ground for both legal and theological viewpoints.

St. Augustine, in his *City of God*, examines this commandment in relation to the suicides of Judas and of

Lucretia, the Roman woman who killed herself for the sake of her chaste honour. Augustine interprets the commandment rigorously. It means simply what it says; it cannot be modified by presuming that God said to Moses, "Thou shalt not kill *others*." Suicide is a form of homicide, just as the law maintained. And as the law can be said to order us to live, so theology commands us to live.

To be consistent with Augustine's interpretation, pacifism and vegetarianism ought also to be the dogma of Christianity. But theology, like law, sanctions some kinds of killing, favouring them over suicide. For instance, the commandment "Thou shalt not kill" is waived for executions, for the slaughter of animals, and for war. Yet, taking one's own life is categorically a sin, and a *sui compotes* (in possession of oneself) suicide is deprived of ecclesiastical burial in the Roman church. But not only the Roman Church; fundamental protestantism, represented by the American Council of Christian Churches, has passed a resolution condemning the Anglican position favouring repeal of the British laws on suicide (1961): "Death by suicide ends all opportunity for repentance. Almighty God created life. It is His. Murder, including self-murder, is a transgression of His law."

Why does theology dread suicide above other forms of killing? Why is theology so exercised?

The theological point of view arises from the idea of the Creation. "Almighty God created life. It is His." We are not our own makers. The sixth commandment follows from the first and second, which place God foremost. We cannot take our lives because they are not ours. They are part of God's creation and we are his creatures. By choosing death, one refuses God's world and denies one's creatureliness. By deciding oneself when the time has come to leave life behind, one exhibits the monstrosity of pride. One has set oneself up in the seat of judgment

31

where God alone may reign over life and death. Suicide is therefore *the* act of rebellion and apostasy for theologians because it denies the very ground of theology itself. Let us look at this.

Theology is the study of God, and the expert in this study is the theologian. The word of theology about God and religion is authoritative. When you or I consider taking our lives, listening in our own ways to God, we no longer follow authority. We set ourselves up as theologians. We are studying God independently. This can well lead to religious delusions and to theological anarchy, with each man having his own God, his own sect, his own theology. Yet, how else is each to find the God immanent, or experience the theological notion that the human soul is the temple of God within? The book of Ecclesiastes states that there is a time to die. If God knows this time, how is man told? *Theology would have us believe that God can speak only through the events of fortune, because death may come only from without.* Again, as with sociology and law, death must be exogenous, visited upon us through the world: enemy, accident, or disease. We do not carry it within us; it resides not in the soul.

But may not God speak through the soul or urge an action through our own hand? Is it not *hubris* from the side of theology to put limits on God's omnipotence that death must always come in the ways which do not threaten the theological root metaphor? For it is not God nor religion that suicide denies, but the claims of theology over death and the way it must be entered. Suicide serves notice on theology by showing that one does not dread its ancient weapons: the hereafter and the last judgment. But it does not follow that suicide because it is anti-theological must be ungodly or irreligious. Cannot suicide prompted from within also be a way for God to announce the time to die? As David Hume wrote in his brief essay

On Suicide: "When I fall upon my own sword, therefore, I receive my death equally from the hands of the Deity as if it has proceeded from a lion, a precipice, or a fever."

Rabbinical thought, and also the precedent of St. Apollonia in the Roman Church, show the way to a religious justification for suicide. Among the early martyrs was one, Apollonia (d. 249), who threw herself into the flames and was sanctified because her death was for God. This was in contradistinction to the host of Christian martyrs who, although going intentionally to slaughter, never raised their own hands against themselves. Suicide as martyrdom was always the Jewish position. Rather than perform under duress the abhorrences of the three greatest sins—idolatry, incest, and murder—suicide is justified. It becomes a form of martyrdom as a sacrifice for the sanctification of God. In other words, even theology can justify suicide when the act is connected to God and has a religious nature. However, theological dogma alone is allowed to decide what is or is not for the sanctification of God. Thus does dogma determine the description of a religious act.

To decide whether an act is merely a theological sin or truly irreligious depends not upon dogma but upon the evidence of the soul. Dogma has already passed its judgment. Since God is not confined by the dogmas of theologies alone, but may, and does, reveal Himself through the soul as well, *it is to the soul one must look for the justification of a suicide*. In other words, the analyst cannot expect help from the theologian, but is turned back to meet the problem on his own ground.

Lastly, let us turn to medicine and the physician. The primary caution of the physician is *primum nihil nocere*—above all, to harm nothing. His tasks are to prevent illness; to treat, heal, and cure where possible; to comfort always; to repair and encourage; to allay pain; to discover and fight disease—all in order to promote physical well-being, that is, life. Anything against these aims must be opposed, because it endangers the root metaphor: promoting life. Where these aims themselves conflict with one another, as for instance where repairing may induce pain, or harming heal, or the comfort of morphine induce disease, a hierarchy of aims is set up. But always *first in this hierarchy is the promotion of life.*

The measure of success of a medical treatment, that is, whether the promotion of life is taking place or not, is judged by physical behaviour. The physician relies mainly upon quantitative standards of activity, such as pulse rate, temperature, basal metabolism, blood count and pressure, as well as refined analyses of secretion and performance. For medicine the promotion of life is organic life, the life of the body. He interprets his rule, *primum nihil nocere,* in terms of the body, asking whether his actions help or harm physical life. The effect of a treatment upon the psyche is not his principal concern in the hierarchy of aims.

Therefore, in the name of this end—promoting life— the physician may be justified to use any means to prevent a patient from taking his life. It is not really the physician's concern should the measures used to capture, calm, isolate, and make accessible for interview a person bent on self-destruction destroy aspects of that self which the physician is trying to aid. The medical model itself supports the standard rule: any indication of suicide, any threat of death, calls for the immediate action of locks and drugs and constant surveillance—treatment usually reserved for criminals.

The modern physician is not expected to concern himself with the soul of his patient, except where the patient's psyche interferes with physical health. Psychological remedies are not recommended for themselves as ends in themselves, but are means for serving the physician's idea of good physiological functioning. He would reduce to a minimum the interference of the psyche in the smooth functioning of a healthy physiological system. The physician would agree that this physiological well-being has as its eventual purpose the sound basis for general well-being —cultural, social, psychological. But his focus remains on the immediate promotion of life, and like a good gardener he pays attention to the material conditions out of which may flower psychic growth.

His task is not with this psychic growth, nor with evaluating his actions in terms of the psyche. His measurement of success depends altogether upon the measurement of body functions. Nothing can be measured unless it be quantified. The representation of medical measure, the one that sums up medicine's highest achievements in promoting life, is the life-expectancy curve. *Promoting life has come to mean prolonging life.* When a patient is 'getting better' it means he is 'living longer'. Improvement is quantitative, and medicine is led to the equation: good life = more life.

But life can be prolonged only at the expense of death. Promoting life therefore also means postponing death. Death, as the one condition for which medicine has no cure, is the arch-enemy of the entire structure. Suicide, which ends the medical life of the patient, then becomes the primary condition to be combated. When serving the patient's life, the physician now tends to serve only one aspect of it—its length. Even its comfort ultimately serves this end, because the physician is obliged to postpone death with every weapon he can command. Yet, willy-nilly, the healthiest life of the finest body moves daily towards its death.

With this interpretation of his task to promote life, with this relative disinterest in the psychological effects of his action, how can the physician take up the problem of suicide objectively? His obligation to his profession has him fixed as tightly in a dogma as any theologian defending the articles of his faith. His root metaphor, as it is interpreted today, does not permit him any alternative but to stand for a continuation of physical life at all costs. Suicide shortens life; therefore it cannot promote life. The physician cannot go with the patient into an exploration of death. At any moment the risk of its reality may force him to draw back. *The medical root metaphor commits the physician to a significant and noble point of view, but its limits are reached when faced with the investigation of suicide.* Suicide means death, the arch-enemy. Suicide is prejudged by the medical model of thought. It can be understood medically only as a symptom, an aberration, an alienation, to be approached with the point of view of prevention.

The models from which those four fields having most to do with suicide regard the problem are of no help to the analyst. All of them prejudge suicide, partly because suicide threatens the root metaphors upon which they stand. Therefore, all share certain traits in common. Their main concern is with suicide prevention because their models are tinged with a dread of death. This dread arises from their not having adequate place for death within their present models of thought. They conceive death as exogenous to life, not as something lodged in the soul, not as a continuous possibility and choice. By admitting this they would be admitting suicide, thereby threatening their own foundations. Neither Society, nor Law, nor Church, nor Life would then be safe.

From the points of view of sociology, law, theology, and medicine the prevention of suicide is a legitimate aim. It may be correct and necessary in every respect save one:

meeting the suicide risk in those comparatively few individuals in analytical practice. The traditional line is defensible and certainly very old; however, it deserves examination from a point of view altogether outside the fields themselves. Some thinkers have done this, notably Donne, Hume, Voltaire, Schopenhauer, but they are not modern enough. They have lacked the psychological point of view which would take for its target the root metaphors of these fields themselves, rather than argue over their ideas of suicide derived from these metaphors. In other words, is suicide incompatible with the model itself? If so, then suicide prevention is but a disguised form of suicide prejudice, which is in turn based on a fundamental dread of death. If suicide prevention is a prejudgment and an analyst opposes it on the grounds that it does not lead to understanding suicide as a psychological fact, this in no way implies that one is therefore 'for suicide'. Again, *the issue is not for or against suicide, but what it means in the psyche.*

So our task is another: to work out the analytical view. It is enough to conclude here that the analyst cannot borrow his approach from his colleagues, who, though they may support one another, offer no support to an enquiring analyst faced with the suicide possibility in his daily work.

The analytical view will have to arise independently of these four fields because suicide shows this independence of the psyche from society, law, theology, and even from the life of the body. Suicide is such a threat to them not only because it pays no heed to the cautions of their traditions and opposes their root metaphors, but largely because it asserts radically the independent reality of the soul.

CHAPTER III

SUICIDE AND THE SOUL

IT appears that all writers on the problem of suicide agree with Farberow and Shneidman (*The Cry for Help*) that "The first major task of any thoroughgoing scientific study of suicide is the development of a taxonomy or classification of types of suicides". And so there is by now an immensely muddled terminology about suicides. They are named pathological, or panic, or altruistic, or anomic, or egotistic, or passive, or chronic, or submeditated, or religious, or political, and so on. Correlations are made between suicide and atmospheric pressure, sunspots, seasonal and economic fluctuations, and also between suicide and biological conditions such as heredity, pregnancy, and menstruation. Suicide is studied in relation to tuberculosis, leprosy, alcoholism, syphilis, psychosis, diabetes. There are publications on suicides in school, in the army, in prison, etc. Statistical surveys make classifications in terms of rates of suicide per hundred thousand persons, by age, sex, religion, race, region. Cultural investigations show variations in attitude towards suicide in different times and countries, and changes in the kinds and frequencies of suicide according to changes in historical periods and philosophies of culture.

We can read of suicides in crowds: of maniacal dancers in fourteenth-century Central Europe, of villagers rushing *en masse* into the flames in seventeenth-century Russia, of girls flinging themselves into the Mihara-Yama volcano in twentieth-century Japan. We know of plunges from lover's leaps, from special bridges, churches, monuments, and towers. Entire towns, sects, and companies have died to the last man rather than surrender. We know of the Christian martyrs of whom John Donne wrote: "Many were baptized only because they would be burnt", so certainly was martyrdom the road to Heaven. The Bible tells of Samson, who said, "Let me die with the Philistines", as he pulled down the house upon himself and his enemies; and it tells of Judas, that first modern man, who "went and hanged himself". We can read this, but what do we understand? How does it help an analyst?

Or, turning to individuals, we find reports of every sort: Petronius, opening and closing his veins at pleasure in the true Epicurean style, exchanged gossip with his friends as he let out his blood for the last time; Seneca and Socrates, out of favour, were their own executioners; antiquity reports the suicides of Hero in the Hellespont, Sappho from the rock at Neritos, Cleopatra, Jocasta the mother and wife of Oedipus, Portia who would follow Brutus, and Paulina after Seneca; more recently, Hart Crane, Herbert Silberer, Thomas Beddoes, Cesare Pavese, Virginia Woolf, and such men of rank and action as Condorcet, Castlereagh, Forrestal, Winant, Vargas, Hemingway, Bridgman the Nobel Laureate, and Belmonte the matador.

What are we to make of these: a daughter of Karl Marx, a son of Eugene O'Neill, of Thomas Mann, of Robert Frost, of Herman Melville?

And how to regard the hundreds of children who take their own lives each year—children neither psychotic, retarded, nor depraved, and some less than ten years old?

Again, will setting up our own descriptive classification, our own sort of morphology, lead us further? For example, let us propose *collective* suicides in the form of the panic death of an animal swarm, the heroic charge of a brigade, or the ritual suicide of *suttee*. Also collective would be the suicides of those employed to die as the political assassin or *kamikaze* pilot; *harakiri* or *seppuku* (belly-cutting) of Japanese men—for women throat-slitting is prescribed; and the extraordinary amount of suicides among the Ardjiligjuar Eskimos (a rate sixty times greater than Canada as a whole).

Another grouping would be the *symbolic* suicides. These may be carried out in bizarre fashion in public, as the exhibitionist Peregrinus on a perfumed pyre before the roaring crowds of the Olympic Games. They may be more schizoid in pattern, such as the suicide of one who immolates his body, symbolically following an archetypal model of dismemberment or religious martyrdom. Some have an obsessive-compulsive quality. The insistency of the drive differs hardly from that of the alcoholic to drink and the addict to drugs. The individual is overpowered by the urge to find his own special symbolic death; and every possible sort has been reported: drinking phenol, eating glass or poisonous spiders, dousing oneself in kerosene and setting fire, lighting the fuse of a swallowed firecracker, creeping into a lion's cage. . . .

Still others we could group together as *emotional* suicides, performed under the domination of an overriding passion. Here would belong revenge against one's enemies, to give others anguish; to manipulate the world, in rage at frustration; humiliation over financial ruin, shame over public exposure; suicides of guilt and conscience, of anxious terror, of the melancholy of ageing, of loneliness, of abandonment, of grief, of apathy and emptiness, of drunken despair and despair over failure, especially failure in love. And here would belong the suicides of success, the leap from the pinnacle. Emotional, too, is the suicidal cry for help "rescue me", and the suicidal urge to kill and to be killed, or the swooning union of the love-death and the self-immolation of an *imitatio dei*, as well as the suicides to avoid physical suffering from torture or disease, or imprisonment, or capture in war.

Then what of the *intellectual* suicides, where loyalty to a cause, principle, or group is the reason? Here we would have to classify the hunger strike and the ascetic suicide that leads to Nirvana and the deaths from martyrdom from which the early Fathers of the Church would countenance no escape. So, too, perhaps the deaths of Socrates and Seneca, as well as suicides of nihilism, rebellion, and absurdity.

The broad conclusion that the analyst can draw from these varied accounts is: suicide is one of the human possibilities. Death can be chosen. The meaning of this choice is different according to the circumstances and the individual. Just here, where the reports and classifications end, the analytical problem begins. An analyst is concerned with the individual meaning of a suicide, which is not given in classifications. An analyst works from the premise that each death is meaningful and somehow understandable, beyond the classification. His approach to a suicide is the same as to any other form of behaviour which coems within his purview, such as the bizarre symptoms called schizophrenic or the functional disorders called psychosomatic. He assumes that behaviour has a meaningful 'inside' and that by getting inside the problem he will be able to understand its meaning.

This approach is psychological. Or, we can say, the soul is its first premise or root metaphor. By claiming distinctions in meaning for each suicide even where outer behaviour is strikingly typical and sociologically classifiable, an analyst makes a claim for an understandable and individual personality to which the suicide can be related and thus understood. He attributes intentionality to every human event. His quest is for meanings.

41

Outer behaviour is generally typical. From the outside each death is merely Death. It always looks the same and can be defined exactly by medicine and by law. When suicide is a description of behaviour and defined as self-destruction, or the initiation of any act the outcome of which is believed by the agent to result in self-destruction, all suicides are Suicide. The individual person who has chosen this death has become 'a suicide'. When death is viewed from the outside, what place remains for the individual soul and its experience of this death? What has it meant? What has happened to tragedy and where is death's sting?

The more scientific the study of suicide becomes, the more it must be viewed from the outside. For this reason, classification is such a trap in psychiatry, sociology, or any of those fields whose main concern should be with understanding human behaviour. Example of the shift from inside to outside can be found in the work of Shneidman, whose leadership in suicide research is taken for granted. He and his co-workers, in their fascination with taxonomy, purposely replace the words 'suicide' and 'death' with 'self-destruction', 'termination', 'cessation', 'Psyde'—all words purged of emotion, purified of psychological life. For all their research, their clues to suicide from case studies and diagnostic classifications yield trivia. Their analysis of suicide notes, by concluding that false reasoning ("confused suicidal logic") is responsible and that suicide is a "psychosemantic fallacy" would be a Joycean parody of research, were it not so sad, so sick, and so typical of psychology's science-complex.

Yet, all fields of enquiry must view phenomena from the outside. Otherwise, they could make no generalisations and there could be no useful terms as suicide and death. Besides, it can be argued that one cannot get 'inside' anything truly, and that there will always remain a

42

'cut' between subject and object. Without groupings and classifications from the outside, each act would be unique; we could make no predictions, record no knowledge, learn nothing. Major issues in psychological practice—delinquency, alcoholism, psychopathy, ageing, homosexuality—are concepts formed in this way. The very word, 'neurosis', with all its forms, symptoms, and mechanisms, is an 'outside' term overriding individual differences. *The concern of an analyst is to maintain his connection with the inside and not to lose his root metaphor.* Else he begins to see his patients as examples of categories and becomes occupied with solving delinquency, psychopathy, homosexuality, and so forth, whereas his calling is to the soul of individuals who exhibit typical traits in their outer behaviour. Outside typicality does not mean a corresponding similarity of experience. 'Alcoholics', 'delinquents', 'psychopaths' do not experience their typical forms of behaviour in the same way. The intentionality of the actions differs in different people. The literature of suicide, only a compressed reference to which we gave above, shows an exhaustive variety of circumstance and purpose which cannot be said to correspond with the typical forms of outer behaviour called suicide by drowning or depressive suicide or suicide while the balance of mind was disturbed.

Jung alone among the great psychologists refused to classify people into groups according to their sufferings. He has been charged with failing to provide a detailed and systematic theory of neurosis along with etiology and treatment. Is this really a failing? Perhaps it is his virtue to have alone recognised the gross inadequacy of only outside descriptions.

An analyst faces problems, and these problems are not merely classifiable behavioural acts, nor medical categories of disease. *They are above all experiences and sufferings,*

43

problems with an 'inside'. The first thing that the patient wants from an analyst is to make him aware of his suffering and to draw the analyst into his world of experience. Experience and suffering are terms long associated with soul. 'Soul', however, is not a scientific term, and it appears very rarely in psychology today, and then usually with inverted commas as if to keep it from infecting its scientifically sterile surround. 'Soul' cannot be accurately defined, nor is it respectable in scientific discussion as scientific discussion is now understood. There are many words of this sort which carry meaning, yet which find no place in today's science. It does not mean that the references of these words are not real because scientific method leaves them out. Nor does it mean that scientific method fails because it omits these words which lack operational definition. All methods have their limits; we need but keep clear what belongs where.

To understand 'soul' we cannot turn to science for a description. Its meaning is best given by its context, and this context has already been partly stated. The root metaphor of the analyst's point of view is that human behaviour is understandable because it has an inside meaning. The inside meaning is suffered and experienced. It is understood by the analyst through sympathy and insight. All these terms are the everyday empirical language of the analyst and provide the context for and are expressions of the analyst's root metaphor. Other words long associated with the word 'soul' amplify it further: mind, spirit, heart, life, warmth, humanness, personality, individuality, intentionality, essence, innermost, purpose, emotion, quality, virtue, morality, sin, wisdom, death, God. A soul is said to be 'troubled', 'old', 'disembodied', 'immortal', 'lost', 'innocent', 'inspired'. Eyes are said to be 'soulful', for the eyes are 'the mirror of the soul'; but one can be 'soulless' by showing no mercy. Most 'primitive' languages have

44

elaborate concepts about animated principles which ethnologists have translated by 'soul'. For these peoples, from ancient Egyptian to modern Eskimo, 'soul' is a highly differentiated idea referring to a reality of great impact. The soul has been imaged as the inner man, and as the inner sister or spouse, the place or voice of God within, as a cosmic force in which all humans, even all things living, participate, as having been given by God and thus divine, as conscience, as a multiplicity and as a unity in diversity, as a harmony, as a fluid, as fire, as dynamic energy, and so on. One can 'search one's soul' and one's soul can be 'on trial'. There are parables describing possession of the soul by and sale of the soul to the Devil, of temptations of the soul, of the damnation and redemption of the soul, of development of the soul through spiritual disciplines, of journeys of the soul. Attempts have been made to localise the soul in specific body organs and regions, to trace its origin to sperm or egg, to divide it into animal, vegetable, and mineral components, while the search for the soul leads always into the 'depths'.

As well, arguments continue on the connection of the soul with the body: that they are parallel; that the soul is an epiphenomenon of the body, a sort of internal secretion; that the body is only the throbbing visibility of an immaterial form-giving soul; that their relation is irrational and synchronistic, coming and going, fading and waxing, in accordance with psychoid constellations; that there is no relation at all; that the flesh is mortal and the soul eternal, reincarnating by karma through the aeons; that each soul is individual and perishable, while it is the body as matter which cannot be destroyed; that soul is only present in sentient bodies possible of consciousness; or, that souls, like monads, are present in all bodies as the psychic hierarchy of nature alive.

From the points of view of logic, theology, and science,

these statements are to be proved and disputed. From the point of view of psychology, *they are one and all true positions, in that they are statements about the soul made by the soul.* They are the soul's description of itself in the language of thought (just as the soul images itself in contradictions and paradoxes in the language of poetry and painting). This implies that at different moments each of these statements reflects a phase of the body–soul relationship. At one time it is synchronistic where everything falls in place. At another time soul and body are so identified, as in toxic states or disease, that epiphenomenalism is the true position. Or at another time, the life-course of body and soul are radically independent and parallel. We must then conclude that such statements about the soul reflect the state of soul of the one making the statement. They reveal the special bent of a person's own psyche-soma problem, a problem that seems unendingly bound up with psychology and the riddle of the soul, since it is this question—what have the body and soul to do with each other —that the soul is continually putting to us in philosophy, religion, art, and above all in the trials of daily life and death.

This exploration of the word shows that we are not dealing with something that can be defined; and therefore, 'soul' is really not a concept, but a symbol. Symbols, as we know, are not completely within our control, so that we are not able to use the word in an unambiguous way, even though we take it to refer to that unknown human factor which makes meaning possible, which turns events into experiences, and which is communicated in love. *The soul is a deliberately ambiguous concept resisting all definition in the same manner as do all ultimate symbols which provide the root metaphors for the systems of human thought.* 'Matter' and 'nature' and 'energy' have ultimately the same ambiguity; so too have 'life', 'health', 'justice', 'society', and 'God', which provide the symbolic sources for the points of view we have already seen. Soul is not more an obfuscation than other axiomatic first principles. Despite modern man's unease with the term, it continues to stand behind and influence the point of view of depth psychology in ways which many depth psychologists themselves might be surprised to discover.

What a person brings to the analytical hour are the sufferings of the soul; while the meanings discovered, the experiences shared, and the intentionality of the thera-peutic process are all expressions of a living reality which cannot be better apprehended than by the root metaphor of psychology, psyche or soul.

The terms 'psyche' and 'soul' can be used inter-changeably, although there is a tendency to escape the ambiguity of the word 'soul' by recourse to the more biological, more modern 'psyche'. 'Psyche' is used more as a natural concomitant to physical life, perhaps reducible to it. 'Soul', on the other hand, has meta-physical and romantic overtones. It shares frontiers with religion.

In short, the root metaphor of the soul, despite its imprecision and complexities, informs the attitudes of the analyst and governs his point of view. When the analyst tries to understand an experience, he attempts to get at its relevance for the soul of the person concerned. Judging a death only from the outside limits understanding. Sartre even maintains that we can never grasp death at all be-cause it is always the death of someone else; we are always outside it. Therefore, enquiries into suicide turn more and more to the psychological autopsy, i.e., individual case studies, to get closer to a psychological point of view. The examination of suicide notes, interviews with attempted suicides, and sociological case studies all try to bring the enquirer closer to the meaning of the death, closer to an understanding of the event from within.

Nevertheless, these investigations remain fundamentally outside because they are investigations made for the sake of information about suicide. They are not investigations made about this or that person's soul with which suicide was meaningfully interwoven. Studies of this sort are carried on in order to get at the causes of suicide and to explain the suicidal drive. With an explanation won through this investigation of the 'suicide problem', treatment can be worked out for 'suicide prevention'. The analyst can then be given recommendations based on statistical evidence, personality profiles, interviews in depth, etc., with which he can meet the 'suicide threat'. The major work of Ringel in Austria, Farberow and Shneidman in the United States, and Stengel in England all proceed along these lines. They aim at suicide prevention. Their explanations and recommendations serve this end.

Because prevention is their goal they cannot adequately serve an analyst. His task is to be objective towards the phenomena of the soul, taking the events as they come without prior judgment. This is his form of scientific openness. The collective points of view—sociological, medical, legal, theological—have declared suicide something to prevent. With this attitude and dread governing their research, they cut themselves off from understanding the very issue they have set out to explain. Their methodology precludes finding what they are looking for. *If an analyst wants to understand something going on in the soul he may never proceed in an attitude of prevention.*

Not prevention, but confirmation, is the analyst's approach to experience. His desire is to give recognition to the states of the soul which the person concerned is undergoing, so that they may become realised in the personality and be lived consciously. He is there to confirm what is going on—*whatever is going on*. Ideally, he is not there to approve, to blame, to alter, or to prevent. He may search for meaning, but this is to explore the given, not to lead away from the experience as it is. Leading away from experience leads also away from understanding the data as they are presented.

Therefore, an analyst is obliged to set aside even the most apparently useful studies on suicide in order to be open to what is immediately at hand. Anything that interferes with his unique emotional understanding of the individual will work against understanding in general. Only that knowledge of which he can make use serves understanding. But suicide knowledge coming from contemporary sources tends not to serve understanding because it has pre-judged the question. Explanations from studies which show suicide as the result of confused reasoning degrade what the soul is going through. Explanations fail the seriousness and enormity of the event. The "psychosemantic fallacy" makes sense enough to the person about to kill himself. The analyst's task is to move his understanding inside the other person to where it makes sense.

Understanding is never a collective phenomenon. It is based on sympathy, on intimate knowledge, on participation. It depends upon a communication of souls and is appropriate to the human encounter, whereas explanation belongs to the viewpoint of the natural sciences. Understanding attempts to stay with the moment as it is, while explanation leads away from the present, backwards into a chain of causality or sideways into comparisons. Particular events tend to be viewed as belonging to classes, so that the unique novelty of each event is sacrificed at the altar of general knowledge.

49

The contrast of viewpoints—understanding from the inside and explaining from the outside—cuts psychology in two. It is an old problem in the history of thought. Any psychology which gives its account of human nature from the outside through observed behaviour only, with explanatory models based on physiology, laboratory experiment, mechanics, sociological statistics, etc., will come to different conclusions from the second kind. Psychology that gives its account through understanding from the inside will use different procedures and concepts and a different starting point—that of the individual. The differences in point of view must be kept in mind by an analyst, *else he will mistakenly try to gain understanding through the study of explanations.* He will try to develop his position to a suicide through the study of the literature rather than through his first-hand observations on and communication with his and the other's psyche. He will fall back upon empty explanatory concepts: "masochism", "self-destructive tendencies", "internalised aggression", "partial suicide", "death wishes", "primary regression", and the like. Although he finds reaction patterns and discovers mechanisms, he loses the soul.

Depth psychology rediscovered the soul and placed it in the centre of its explorations. Now it runs the risk of losing it again under pressure from academic psychology. Academic psychology, in its eagerness to be as scientific as physics, has one-sidedly chosen the 'outside', so that the soul no longer finds a place in the only field dedicated by its very name to its study. Hence, depth psychology has been more or less kept out of the academies of official psychology. To enter, it is asked to yield its viewpoint, its language, and its discoveries. It is asked to prove by experimental methods its clinical findings. It must translate clinical understanding into an alien tongue of natural science explanation. In short, the price of admission is loss of soul. But without a psychology which investigates in depth the individual soul for meaning, there is no way to understand problems such as suicide that plague official psychology. Depth psychology is the stone the builders of the academy have rejected. It may one day have to become the keystone of any truly scientific psychology, because the understanding of human nature must begin with the soul and use methods most suited to the object of study. Psychology means 'logos of psyche', the speech or telling of the soul. As such, psychology is necessarily depth psychology, since, as we have seen above, soul refers to the inner, the deep. And the logic of psychology is necessarily the method of understanding which tells of the soul and speaks to the soul in its own language. *The deeper a psychology can go with its understanding,* i.e., *into universal inner meanings expressed by the archetypal speech of mythical 'tellings', the more scientifically accurate it is on the one hand and the more soul it has on the other.*

In order to get closer to the problem of suicide, we first try to understand the life of the individual whose death is involved. We begin with an individual, not with the concept. The individual's personality is, of course, partly conscious and partly unconscious, so that an enquiry into the unconscious aspects of the individual also becomes necessary. In fact, an enquiry which does not give full share to the inner mythology (as dreams, fantasies, apperceptional modes) of the suicidal individual will give an inadequate picture. All the reasons for suicide mentioned at the beginning of this chapter—collective, emotional, intellectual—do not penetrate below the surface, do not get inside the death. Because suicide is a way of entering death and because the problem of entering death releases the most profound fantasies of the human soul, *to understand a suicide we need to know what mythic fantasy is being enacted.* Again, it is an analyst who is in the best position to gain this fuller understanding.

However, this has been contested. The opposition to psychological understanding of individual suicides comes not only from the 'outside' position of sociology. (We have already seen the argument: it is useless to delve into the units which happen to make up the suicide quotient.) Opposition comes as well from the 'inside'. According to Sartre, the one person best able to understand a death is the person who is dead. This means that suicide is incomprehensible because the one person who might give an account no longer can. This is a false dilemma, and we must look more closely at the extreme inside position. We must see whether or not it is true that each individual is the only one who can understand and articulate his own life and death.

The articulate suicide, Socrates or Seneca, is rare. A man who understands his own myth, who is able to follow his pattern so clearly that he can sense the moment of his death and tell of it, is unusual in human history. These are the very few. Their awareness has turned them into legends. The ordinary man has little understanding of his actions, and *because death usually takes him by surprise, it seems to come from without.* Because we are so little connected to the death we carry within us, it seems to strike exogenously as an outer force. Always, what we are unconscious of in ourselves seems to come from without. We do our best to bring fragments of our actions to awareness, but we are more often lived by than live our myth. The best example of our helplessness in understanding and articulating our inner life is the problem we have with our dreams.

It takes two to interpret a dream. Unless there is a codified system, as, say, in the old Egyptian dream book of Horapollo or in the modern one of the Freudians, a dream is a riddle. Bits of its message come through to some by instinct, to others by training. But the tale cannot be unravelled either by the analysand alone or by the analyst alone. It is a dialectical process; *understanding needs a mirror*. The more an analyst is 'inside' the case, is familiar with the other's soul as its mirror, the better he can understand the dream. So, too, with suicide. But if he is too close—and this is what is meant by counter-transference identification—he can no longer reflect because he has then become too much like the other. He and the other have become unconscious together in the same place. The mirror darkens and the dialectic is gone. An analyst needs to have one foot in and one foot out. This position is unique to the analytical relationship. Its achievement is intensely difficult, which accounts for the years of personal analysis and training required for the profession. It is a discipline comparable to that of science, and the objectivity acquired is different from but equivalent to the objectivity in the natural sciences. We shall discuss it more fully in the second part of this book.

Being both 'in' and 'out' means that an analyst is in a better position to understand and to articulate the psychology of another person. He can follow the pattern because he is at once in it and observing it, while the other person is usually only in it and caught by it. *He is thus able to understand a suicide better than the one who commits it.* The person dead, contrary to Sartre, is not the one having a privileged access to his own death, because part of the meaning of this death was always unconscious to him. It could only have become conscious through the dialectical mirror, a process for which an analyst has been trained.

Where an analyst's understanding may have the effect of prevention, this understanding may not lead to explanation, or give information to others which may be useful in their search for causes and prevention. He understands by appreciating the condition of the soul at the time of death, but owing to the unique relationship his understanding and its articulation cannot be verified by proof. He is alone.

This isolated situation is the crux of viewing the problem from the soul and gives analysis its creatively lonely mission. Like the person whose suicide is not understood by the collective, or interpreted only in terms of conscious motives or alien systems of thought, an analyst's understanding of the suicide is also not understood by the collective. Understanding is not a collective phenomenon. Psychology still awaits the day when this understanding can be explained. Alone of the vocations dealing with human nature and the soul, analysis has no position other than the soul. There is no authority higher than the analysis itself, no medical, legal, or theological point of repair to outside positions which resist death and seek its prevention.

Rules for judging whether a suicide—or any event in analysis—is justified cannot be summarily stated. To do so would be to forsake the inside for the outside. It would mean we are no longer trying to understand the individual event in its uniqueness, but are looking at forms of behaviour, classes of acts. However, this emphasis upon understanding does not mean *tout comprendre, tout pardonner*. Understanding does not mean standing by in sympathetic non-directive acceptance no matter what happens. An analyst has his criteria for justification. These criteria are derived mainly from *an assessment of the conscious mind at the time of death in its relation to objective processes of the unconscious which form the archetypal substructure of behaviour*. Hence, analytical understanding requires knowledge of these objective psychic processes. The knowledge required in meeting the suicide risk is paradoxically about the great unknowable, death. This knowledge is not medical, legal, or theological, which consists anyway of abstractions. It is rather knowledge about the *experience* of death, the archetypal background of death as met in the soul, its meanings, images, and emotions, its import in psychic life, so that one can try to understand the experiences undergone during the suicidal crisis. An analyst makes judgments and tries to operate with an exactitude and an ethic as do other scientists. Nor does he differ from other scientists when he takes his criteria from only his own field.

How an analyst might understand the death experience and proceed in face of suicide we shall soon come to. Here we have tried to delimit the model upon which the analyst stands from other models which are not authentic to his calling. When he steps outside the soul and takes his criteria from theological, sociological, medical, or legal morality, he performs as a layman and his opinions are lay opinions, no longer scientific judgments based on his disciplined training and the psychological material under observation. As a man he is indeed tied to the actualities of life. He is involved with society, law, church, and physical reality. Even his profession has become collectively recognised and imbued with trust—but only because this profession has been conceived on the inauthentic model of medicine. His vocation is to the soul as it is in individual human beings. This calling places him in a vacuum with his patient where, paradoxically, the obligations of the collective which gave him professional recognition are suspended.

But as long as an analyst is true to the psyche he is not lay. He has his ground, and this ground has place for death.

CHAPTER IV

THE DEATH EXPERIENCE

PSYCHOLOGY has not paid enough attention to death. How little literature there is compared with those earnest annotated studies on the trivia of life. The examination of death through the study of the soul is surely one of psychology's prime tasks. But psychology can never take it up until it has freed itself from its sense of inferiority regarding the other sciences which tend, because of their models of thought, to turn away from this enquiry. Were psychology to start from psychotherapy, thereby putting the actual psyche in the centre of its interest, it would be forced to face the problem of death before any of those other topics which consume so much academic talent.

Is academic psychology's avoidance of death only for reasons of science, only because death is not a subject for empirical investigation? Sleep, death's symbolic counter-part, is also neglected in modern psychology. As Webb points out, studies of sleeping (and dreaming, too) are scant in proportion to other research. Could the relative disinterest of academic psychology in dreaming, sleeping, and dying be further witness to its loss of soul and dread of death?

Theology has always known that death is the soul's first concern. Theology is in a sense devoted to death, with its sacraments and funeral rites, its eschatological elaborations and its descriptions of Heavens and Hells. But death itself is hardly open to theological enquiry. The canons have been laid down by articles of faith. The authority of priesthoods draws its strength from canons which represent a worked-out position towards death.

The position may vary from religion to religion, but it is always there. The theologian knows where he stands about death. Scripture, tradition, and office tell him why there is death and what is expected of him in regard to it. The anchor of the theologian's psychology, and his authority, is his doctrine about life-after-death. Theological proofs for the existence of the soul are so bound to canons of death—canons about immortality, sin, resurrection, last judgment—that an open enquiry brings into question the very basis of theological psychology. The theological position, we must remember, begins at the end opposite to the psychological one. It starts from dogma, not data; from crystallised, not living, experience. Theology requires a soul to provide ground for the elaborate death-belief system which is part of its power. Were there no soul, one might expect theology to invent one in order to authorise the priesthoods' ancient prerogatives on death.

The viewpoint of the natural sciences, including medicine, is more like that of theology. It is a fixed position towards death. This view shows signs of modern mechanism; death is simply the last of a chain of causes. It is an end-state of entropy, a decomposition, a stillness. Freud conceived the death drive in this way because he worked from the base of the natural sciences of the last century. Images of dying, such as running down, cooling, slowing, stiffening, fading, all show death as the last stage of decay. Death is the final link in the process of ageing.

When we look at nature this point of view seems correct. Death shows decay and quiescence. The vegetable world falls into silence following ripeness and the production of seed. Death completes a cycle. Any death previous to the full cycle is obviously premature. When suicide is called 'unnatural' this means that suicide goes against the vegetable cycle of nature which human nature also shares. Surprisingly, however, we know little about the vegetable cycle, which shows varying patterns of senescence and dying. The genetics of ageing in cells, what is a natural time-span, the role of environmental (including radiation) factors remain biological puzzles, especially as we go higher in the scale of species complexity. According to Leopold, explanations in this field are remarkably few. Is this again a sign of the dread of death influencing scientific enquiry? Medical notions of suicide as 'premature' and 'unnatural' cannot find much support from biological research because we do not know to what these terms refer even in the vegetable world. Furthermore, all judgments about life processes other than human ones are made from the outside, so that we must think ourselves strenuously away from natural science metaphors. They can never be fully valid for human life and death, which take their meaning only from the fact that they have an inside. It is from this inside perspective that all questions of 'natural' and 'appropriate' will have to be answered.

On the face of it, those who attempt suicide in order to find a vegetative stillness before the completion of their round are cutting life unnaturally short. But this is how it looks from the outside. We do not know what complexities set off senescence and death in plants and we know less about a 'natural cycle' or span of years in man. We do not know at what point in a longevity curve each life is statistically supposed to enter death. We do not know what bearing time has upon death. We do not know whether the soul dies at all.

Neither theology, nor medical science, but a third field, philosophy, comes nearest to formulating the analyst's experiences of death. Said first by Plato (*Phaedo* 64), repeated in other places at other times, exaggerated, contested, torn from context, the philosophers' maxim holds true: philosophy is the pursuit of death and dying. The old natural philosopher, who was usually both physician and philosopher, pondered with the skull upon his table. Not only did he see death from the viewpoint of life. He viewed life through the sockets of the skull.

Life and death come into the world together; the eyes and the sockets which hold them are born at the same moment. *The moment I am born I am old enough to die.* As I go on living I am dying. Death is entered continuously, not just at the moment of death as legally and medically defined. Each event in my life makes its contribution to my death, and I build my death as I go along day by day. The counter position must logically also follow: any action aimed against death, any action which resists death, hurts life. Philosophy can conceive life and death together. For philosophy they need not be exclusive opposites, polarised into Freud's Eros and Thanatos, or Menninger's Love against Hate, one played against the other. One long tradition in philosophy puts the matter in quite another way. Death is the only absolute in life, the only surety and truth. Because it is the only condition which all life must take into account, it is the only human *a priori*. Life matures, develops, and aims at death. Death is its very purpose. We live in order to die. Life and death are contained within each other, complete each other, are understandable only in terms of each other. Life takes on its value through death, and the pursuit of death is the kind of life philosophers have often recommended. If only the living can die, only the dying are really alive.

Modern philosophy has come again to death, a main current of its tradition. Through the problem of death, philosophy and psychology are rejoining. Freud and Jung, Sartre and Heidegger, have placed death in the middle of their works. Most of Freud's followers rejected his metapsychology of death. Yet today, psychotherapy is fascinated with Heidegger, whose central theme is a metaphysics of death. Heidegger's Germanic language borne on a Black Forest wind is not what interests analysts. Nor is his logic of use, because it does not correspond with psychological facts. When he says that death is the fundamental possibility yet cannot be experienced as such, he is but repeating the rationalist arguments that existence and death (being and not-being) are logical contraries: where I am death is not, where death is I am not. Bridgman (who committed suicide in his old age) reasons in the same way: "There is no operation by which I can decide whether I am dead; 'I am always alive'." This line of thinking is taken by those who have trouble separating the realm of psychological experience from the realm of mentation or rational consciousness. This line argues that dying can be experienced, but not death. If we follow along we are led into foolishness, for we will have to say sleep and the unconscious can also not be experienced. Such quibbles no more affect psychological experience than do logical oppositions obtain in the soul.

Death and existence may exclude each other in rational philosophy, but they *are not psychological contraries*. Death can be experienced as a state of being, an existential condition. The very old sometimes inform us of experiences of finding themselves in another world which is not only more real but from which they view this. In dreams and in psychosis one can go through the anguish of dying, or one is dead; one knows it and feels it. In visions, the dead return and report on themselves. Every analysis shows death experiences in all variety, and we shall turn to examples shortly. The experience of death cannot be forced into a logical definition of death. What gives Heidegger—that unpsychological man—his influence in psychotherapy is one crucial insight. He confirms Freud by placing death at the centre of existence. *And analysts cannot get on without a philosophy of death.*

But philosophers provide answers to questions no more than analysts, or rather they provide many sorts of answers by splitting questions open to reveal many seeds of meaning. An analyst turning towards philosophy will not get the same defined viewpoint towards death and suicide as he will from systems of religion, law, and science. The one answer he will get from philosophy is philosophy itself; for when we ask about death we have begun to practise philosophy, the study of dying. This kind of answer is also psychotherapy.

To philosophise is partly to enter death; philosophy is death's rehearsal, as Plato said. It is one of the forms of the death experience. It has been called "dying to the world". The first movement in working through any problem is taking the problem upon oneself as an experience. One enters an issue by joining it. One approaches death by dying. Approaching death requires a dying in soul, daily, as the body dies in tissue. And as the body's tissue is renewed, so is the soul regenerated through death experiences. Therefore, working at the death problem is both a dying from the world with its illusory sustaining hope that there is no death, not really, and a dying into life, as a fresh and vital concern with essentials.

Because living and dying in this sense imply each other, any act which holds off death prevents life. 'How' to die means nothing less than 'how' to live. Spinoza turned the Platonic maxim around, saying (*Ethics* IV, 67) the philosopher thinks of nothing less than death, but this meditation is not of death but of life. Living in terms of life's only certain end means to live aimed towards death. This end is present here and now as the purpose of life, which means the moment of death—at any moment—is every moment. *Death cannot be put off to the future and reserved for old age.* By the time we are old we may no longer be able to experience death; then it may be merely to go through its outer motions. Or, it may have already been experienced, so that organic death has lost all sting. For organic death cannot undo the fundamental accomplishments of the soul. *Organic death has absolute power over life when death has not been allowed in life's midst.* When we refuse the experience of death we also refuse the essential question of life, and leave life unaccomplished. Then organic death prevents our facing the ultimate questions and cuts off our chance for redemption. To avoid this state of soul, traditionally called damnation, we are obliged to go to death before it comes to us.

Philosophy would tell us that we build towards death from day to day. We build each our own 'ship of death' within ourselves. From this standpoint, by making our own deaths we are killing ourselves daily, so that each death is a suicide. Whether "from a lion, a precipice, or a fever", each death is of our own making. Then we need not beg with Rilke, "O Lord, give each man his own death", since just that God does give us, though we do not see it because we do not like it. When a man builds the structure of his life upwards like a building, climbing step by step, storey by storey, only to go out the high window or to be brought low by heart attack or stroke, has he not fulfilled his own architectural plan and been given his own death? In this view, suicide is no longer one of the ways of entering death, but *all death is suicide,* and the choice of method is only more or less evident, whether car-crash, heart-attack, or those acts usually called suicide.

By consciously going towards death, philosophy says we build the better vessel. Ideally, as we age, this building becomes more incorruptible, so that the passage to it from the failing flesh may be without fear, felicitous and easy. This death we build within us is that permanent structure, the 'subtle body', in which the soul is housed amidst the decay of impermanence. But death is no easy matter; and dying is a rending business, ugly, cruel, and full of suffering. Going towards death consciously as philosophy proposes must therefore be a major human achievement, which is held up to us by the images of our religious and cultural heroes.

An analyst may do well to consider philosophy as a first step in his struggle with the suicide problem. Suicide can be for some an act of unconscious philosophy, an attempt to understand death by joining it. The impulse to death need not be conceived as an anti-life movement; it may be a demand for an encounter with absolute reality, *a demand for a fuller life through the death experience.*

Without dread, without the prejudices of prepared positions, without a pathological bias, suicide becomes 'natural'. It is natural because it is a possibility of our nature, a choice open to each human psyche. The analyst's concern is less with the suicidal choice as such, than it is with helping the other person to understand the meaning of this choice, *the only one which asks directly for the death experience.*

A main meaning of the choice is the importance of death for individuality. As individuality grows so does the possibility of suicide. Sociology and theology recognise this, as we have seen. Where man is law unto himself, responsible to himself for his own actions (as in the culture of cities, in the unloved child, in protestant areas, in creative people), the choice of death becomes a more frequent alternative. In this choice of death, of course, the opposite lies concealed. Until we can choose death, we cannot choose life. *Until we can say no to life, we have not really said yes to it*, but have only been carried along by its collective stream. The individual standing against this current experiences death as the first of all alternatives, for he who goes against the stream of life is its opponent and has become identified with death. Again, the death experience is needed to separate from the collective flow of life and to discover individuality.

Individuality requires courage. And courage has since classic times been linked with suicide arguments: it takes courage to choose the ordeal of life, and it takes courage to enter the unknown by one's own decision. Some choose life because they are afraid of death and others choose death because they are afraid of life. We cannot justly assess courage or cowardice from the outside. But we can understand why the problem of suicide raises these questions of courage, since the suicide issue forces one to find his individual stand on the basic question—to be or not to be. The courage to be—as it is modishly called—means not just choosing life out there. The real choice is choosing oneself, one's individual truth, including the ugliest man, as Nietzsche called the evil within. To continue life, knowing what a horror one is, takes indeed courage. And not a few suicides may arise from an overwhelming experience of one's own evil, an insight coming more readily to the creatively gifted, the psychologically sensitive, and the schizoid. Then who is the coward and who casts the first stone? The rest of us brutish men who go about dulled to our own shadows.

Each analysis comes upon death in one form or another. The dreamer dies in his dreams and there are deaths of other inner figures; relatives die; positions are lost never to be regained; deaths of attitudes; the death of love; experiences of loss and emptiness which are described as death; the sense of the presence of death and the terrible

64

fear of dying. Some are "half in love with easeful death" for themselves or wish it for others, wanting to be killed or to kill. There is death in soaring sunwards like young Ikaros, in climbing for power, in the arrogant ambitions of omnipotence fantasies, where in one stroke of hatred and rage all enemies vanish. Some seem driven to death; others are hounded by it; still others are drawn to it by a call from what can only be empirically described as 'the other side', a longing for a dead lover, or parent, or child. Others may have had an acute mystical vision as an encounter with death which has haunted their lives, forming an un-understood experience towards which they yearn. For some, each separation is death, and parting is dying. There are those who feel cursed, certain their life is an ineluctable progress into doom, a chain of destiny, the last link called suicide. Some may have escaped death in a holocaust or war and not yet have inwardly escaped, and the anxiety is enacted again and again. Phobias, compulsions, and insomnia may reveal a core of death. Masturbation, solitary and against the call of love and, like suicide, called the 'English disease', evokes fantasies of death. Death can impinge upon the moral 'how' of the individual's life: the review of life, one's faith, sins, destiny; how one got to where one is and how to continue. Or, whether to continue.

To understand all these death patterns, analysis cannot turn anywhere but to the soul to see what it says about death. Analysis develops its ideas on death empirically from the soul itself. Again Jung has been the pioneer. He simply listened to the soul tell its experiences and watched the images of the goal of life which the living psyche produces out of itself. Here, he was neither philosopher, nor physician, nor theologian, but psychologist, student of the soul.

He discovered that death has many guises and that it

does not usually appear in the psyche as death *per se*, as extinction, negation, and finality. Images of dying and ideas of death have quite other meanings in dreams and fantasies. The soul goes through many death experiences, yet physical life goes on; and as physical life comes to a close, the soul often produces images and experiences that show continuity. The process of consciousness seems to be endless. *For the psyche, neither is immortality a fact, nor is death an end.* We can neither prove nor disprove survival. The psyche leaves the question open.

Searching for proof and demonstration of immortality is muddled thinking, because proof and demonstration are categories of science and logic. The mind uses these categories and the mind is convinced by proof. That is why the mind can be replaced by machines and the soul not. Soul is not mind and has other categories for dealing with its problem of immortality. For the soul, the equivalents of proof and demonstration are belief and meaning. They are as difficult to develop and make clear, as hard to wrestle with, as is proof. The soul struggles with the after-life question in terms of its experiences. Out of these experiences, not out of dogma or logic or empirical evidence, the positions of faith are built. And the fact alone that the psyche has this faculty of belief, unaffected by proof or demonstration, presses us towards the possibility of psychic immortality. Psychic immortality means neither resurrection of the flesh nor personal after-life. The former refers to immortality of the body, the latter to immortality of the mind. Our concern is with immortality of the soul.

What might be the function of these categories of belief and meaning in the soul? Are they not part of the soul's equipment—as proof and demonstration are used by the mind—for dealing with reality? If so, then the objects of belief may indeed be 'real'. This *psychological argument for immortality* has as its premise the old correspondence idea that the world and the soul of man are intimately linked. The psyche functions in correspondence with objective reality. If the soul has a function of belief it implies a corresponding objective reality for which belief has its function. This psychological position has been stated in the theological arguments that only believers get to Heaven. Without the function of belief, there is no corresponding reality of Heaven.

This psychological approach to immortality can be put another way: following Jung, the concept of energy and its indestructibility was an ancient and widespread notion associated in countless ways with the idea of the soul, long before Robert Mayer formulated the conservation of energy into a scientific law. We cannot get away from this primordial image even in modern scientific psychology, which still speaks of the psyche in dynamic terms. What is immortality and reincarnation of the soul in psychology is conservation and transformation of energy in physics. The mind's certainty that energy is 'eternal' is given by law in physics. This corresponds with the soul's conviction that it is immortal, and the sense of immortality is the inner feeling of the eternity of psychic energy. *For if the psyche is an energetic phenomenon, then it is indestructible.* Its existence in 'another life' cannot be proved any more than the existence of the soul in this life can be proved. Its existence is given only psychologically in the form of inner certainty, i.e., belief.

When we ask why each analysis comes upon the death experience so often and in such variety, we find, primarily, *death appears in order to make way for transformation.* The flower withers around its swelling pod, the snake sheds its skin, and the adult puts off his childish ways. The creative force kills as it produces the new. Every turmoil and disorder called neurosis can be seen as a life and death struggle in which the players are masked. What is called death by the neurotic mainly because it is dark and unknown is a new life trying to break through into consciousness; what he calls life because it is familiar is but a dying pattern he tries to keep alive. The death experience breaks down the old order, and in so far as analysis is a prolonged 'nervous breakdown' (synthesising too as it goes along), *analysis means dying*. The dread to begin an analysis touches these deep terrors, and the fundamental problem of resistance cannot be taken superficially. Without a dying to the world of the old order, there is no place for renewal, because, as we shall consider later, it is illusory to hope that growth is but an additive process requiring neither sacrifice nor death. The soul favours the death experience to usher in change. Viewed this way, a suicide impulse is a transformation drive. It says: 'Life as it presents itself must change. Something must give way. Tomorrow and tomorrow and tomorrow is a tale told by an idiot. The pattern must come to a complete stop. But, since I can do nothing about life out there, having tried every twist and turn, I shall put an end to it here, in my own body, that part of the objective world over which I still have power. I put an end to myself.'

When we examine this reasoning we find it leads from psychology to ontology. The movement towards a complete stop, towards that fulfilment in stasis where all processes cease, is an attempt to enter another level of reality, to move from becoming to being. To put an end to oneself means to come to one's end, to find the end or limit of what one is, in order to arrive at what one is not—yet. 'This' is exchanged for 'that'; one level is wiped out for another. *Suicide is the attempt to move from one realm to another by force through death.*

This movement to another aspect of reality can be

formulated by those basic opposites called body and soul, outer and inner, activity and passivity, matter and spirit, here and beyond, which become symbolised by life and death. The agony over suicide represents the struggle of the soul with the paradox of all these opposites. The suicide decision is a choice between these contradictions which seem impossible to reconcile. Once the choice is made, ambivalence overcome (as the studies of Ringel and of Morgenthaler on suicide notes show), the person is usually deliberate and calm, giving no sign of his intention to kill himself. He has crossed over.

This calm corresponds with the death experience of the physically dying, of whom Sir William Osler said, "A few, very few, suffer severely in the body and fewer still in the mind." The death agony usually takes place before the moment of organic death. Death comes first as an experience of the soul, after which the body expires. "Fear," says Osis, "is not a dominant emotion in the dying", whereas elation and exaltation occur frequently. Other investigations of dying report similar findings. The fear of dying concerns *the experience of death*, which is separable from physical death and not dependent upon it.

If suicide is a transformation impulse we can regard today's concern with mass suicide through the Bomb as an attempt of the collective psyche at renewal by ridding itself of the binds of history and the weight of its material accumulations. In a world where things and the physical life overwhelmingly predominate, where goods have become the 'good', that which would destroy them and us with them because of our attachments will, of course, become 'evil'. Yet, could this evil not somewhere be a good in disguise, by showing how shaky and relative our current values are? Through the Bomb we live in the shadow of death. Where it may bring the death experience nearer, it must not mean that mass suicide is also closer. Where life is clung to, suicide takes on the compulsive attraction of 'over-kill'. But where collective death is lived with—as in the Nazi concentration camps or during war—suicide is seldom. The point is: *the more immanent the death experience, the more possibility for transformation*. The world is closer to a collective suicide, yes; that this suicide must actually occur, no. What must occur if the actual suicide does not come is a transformation in the collective psyche. The Bomb may thus be God's dark hand which He has shown before to Noah and the peoples of the Cities of the Plain, urging not death, but a radical transformation in our souls.

In individuals where the suicide impulse is not directly associated with the ego, but seems a voice or figure or content of the unconscious that pushes or leads or orders the person to self-murder, again it can be saying: "We cannot meet one another again until a change takes place, a change which ends your identification with your concrete life". *Suicide fantasies provide freedom from the actual and usual view of things*, enabling one to meet the realities of the soul. These realities appear as images and voices, as well as impulses, with which one can communicate. But for these conversations with death one must take the realm of the soul—with its night spirits, its uncanny emotions and shapeless voices, where life is disembodied and highly autonomous—as a reality. Then what appear as regressive impulses can reveal their positive values.

For instance, a young man who would hang himself after an examination failure is drawn to choke off his spirit, or blow out his brains, after having tried too hard to fly too high. Death is dark and easeful; passivity and the inertia of matter draw him down again. Melancholy, that black affliction in which so many suicides occur, shows the pull of gravity downwards into the dark, cold bones of reality. Depression narrows and concentrates upon essences, and suicide is the final denial of existence for the sake of essence. Or, a dead father figure (as Hamlet's ghost) continues to fascinate a woman through suicide thoughts. When she turns to face him she finds him saying: "You are lost in the mundane because you have forgotten your father and buried your aspirations. Die and ascend". Even in those suicide notes where a husband kills himself ostensibly to remove the obstacle to his wife's freedom and happiness, there is an attempt to achieve another state of being through suicide. There is an attempt at transformation.

Transformation, to be genuine and thorough, always affects the body. Suicide is always somewhere a body problem. The transformations from infancy to childhood are accompanied by physical changes both in body structure and libidinal zones; so, too, the major transforming moments of life at puberty, menopause, and old age. Crises are emotional, transfusing the body with joy and anguish and altering looks and habit. Initiation rites are ordeals of the flesh. The death experience emphasises transformation in the body and *suicide is an attack on bodily life*. The Platonic idea that the soul was trapped in the body and released by death has relevance here. Some feel themselves alien in their own bodies all their lives. To encounter the realm of the soul as a reality equal to the usual view of reality, a dying to the world is indeed required. This may produce the impulse to destroy the bodily trap. And, because we can never know whether the old idea of immortal soul in mortal body is true or not, the analyst will at least consider suicide in the light of a body–soul opposition.

The attack on bodily life is for some an attempt *to destroy the affective basis of ego-consciousness*. Suicidal mutilations are extreme distortions of this form of the death experience. Such mutilations can be understood in the light of Eastern meditation techniques or in the universal imagery of sacrificing the animal carrier, bodily life. Because images and fantasies impel action, methods are used for killing off the affective impulse from psychological contents. Memory is washed of desire. For action to be purged of impulse and for image to be free for imaginative play and meditative concentration, bodily desire must die. It must not die directly through suicide, which in this case would be a concrete misinterpretation of a psychological necessity. The necessity is simply that, for an awareness beyond egocentric limitations, affect and image must be separated. This separation proceeds through the introversion of the libido, archetypally represented by the incest complex. Then bodily desire unites with the soul, rather than with the world. The affective impulse becomes then wholly psychic through this conjunction and is transformed.

When the psyche persists in presenting its demands for transformation it may use, besides death, other symbols showing birth and growth, transitions of place and time, and the like. Death, however, is the most effective because it brings with it that intense emotion without which no transformation takes place. The death experience challenges most, requiring a vitally whole response. It means all process is stopped. It is the confrontation with tragedy, for there is no way out, except onward, into it. Tragedy is born *in extremis*, where one is cornered into making a *salto mortale* towards another plane of being. Tragedy is the leap out of history into myth; personal life is pierced by the impersonal arrows of fate. *The death experience offers each life the opening into tragedy*, for, as the Romantics saw it, death extinguishes the merely personal and transposes life on to the heroic key where sounds not only adventure, experiment, and absurdity, but more— the tragic sense of life. Tragedy and death are necessarily interwoven, so that the death experience has the bite of tragedy, and the tragic sense is the awareness of death.

The other symbols of transformation (as birth, growth, transitions of place and time) all openly indicate a next stage. They present this next stage before the present one is over. They unfold new possibilities, affording hope; whereas the death experience never feels like a transition. It is the major transition which, paradoxically, says there is no future. The end has come. It is all over, too late.

Under the pressure of 'too late', knowing that life went wrong and there is no longer a way out, suicide offers itself. *Then suicide is the urge for hasty transformation.* This is not premature death, as medicine might say, but the late reaction of a delayed life which did not transform as it went along. It would die all at once, and now, because it missed its death crises before. This impatience and intolerance reflects a soul that did not keep pace with its life; or, in older people, a life that no longer nourishes with experiences a still-hungering soul. For the old there is guilt and sin to be expiated, and so I am my own executioner. The spouse is dead. There may be no certainty about an after-life reunion, yet there may at least be a possibility of joining on the 'other side', whereas here is but barren grief. Or there is the sense of having already died; an apathetic indifference that says, "I don't care if I live or die." The soul has already left a world through which the body moves like painted cardboard. In each case time is out of joint and suicide would set it right.

When analysis presents the death experience it is often associated with those primary images of the soul, the anima and animus. The struggles with the seductions of the anima and the plots of the animus are contests with death. These struggles are more lethal in adult life than

73

are the parental threats of the negative mother and father images. The challenges of the anima and animus threaten even the life of the organism, because the core of these archetypal dominants is psychoid, that is, bound up with the physical life of the body through emotion. Disease, crime, psychosis, and addiction are only some of the crasser manifestations of the death aspects of the anima and animus archetypes. Again and again, the animus appears as the killer and the anima as the temptress who seemingly leads a man into life but only to destroy him. The psychology of Jung offers deep insights into these specific carriers of death in the soul.

In analysis a person finds death all about him, especially in dreams. There he cuts up the old order with knives, burns it, and buries it. Buildings crumble; there is rot, worms, or fire in the walls. He follows funeral processions and enters graveyards. There sounds uncanny music. He sees unknown corpses, watches women at their prayers, and hears the bell toll. His name is inscribed in a family album, a register, or a stone. Parts of his body disintegrate; the surgeon, the gardener, and the executioner come for dismemberment. A judge condemns, a priest performs last rites. A bird lies fallen on its back. It is twelve o'clock, or happenings come in dark threes. Claws, coffins, shrouds, grimacing masks with teeth appear. Scythes, serpents, dogs, bones, white and black horses, ravens portend destruction. A thread is cut, a tree felled. Things go up in smoke. There are signs of gates and thresholds. He is led downward by an ambiguous female; or, if a woman, disembodied eyes, fingers, wings, and voices indicate to her a dark way. Or there can be a marriage, intercourse with an angel, a weird dance, rioting at a wake, an ancestral banquet of symbolic foods, or a journey to a happy paradisical land. A sense of dampness is felt, as of the tomb, and a sudden gust of chill wind.

There is death by air, by fire, by water, and by burial in the earth. Coma, ecstasy, and the trance of effortless passivity float the dreamer away. Or he is caught in a net or a web. He witnesses the death of all the carriers of no longer viable ways of adaptation, as favourites of childhood, world heroes, even as beloved pets and plants and trees. As old relationships fade in daily life there are departures and he loses habitual ways of behaving, he finds himself a hermit in a cave, by a stagnant pool, in the desert thirsting, at the abyss edge, or on a far island. Again, he is threatened by forces of nature (the sea or lightning) chased by packs of animals, of murderers (robbers and ravishers), or sinister machines. Or, he may turn upon himself.

The varieties of imagery for experiencing death would seem unlimited. Each tells the way the conscious view of death is reflected by the unconscious, ranging from sweet escape to brutal murder. Each time that one experiences these images and a new turn of suffering begins, a piece of life is being given over and we go through loss, mourning, and grief. With it comes loneliness and a vacuum. Each time something has come to a stop.

Where the death experience insists on a suicidal image, then it is the patient's 'I' and everything he holds to be his 'I' which is coming to its end. The entire network and structure is to be broken, every tie slipped, every bond loosed. The 'I' will be totally and unconditionally released. The life that has been built up is now a cage of commitments to be sprung; for a man it is often with the violence of masculine force and for a woman a dissolution into the soft reception of nature through drowning, asphyxiation, or sleep. What comes next no longer matters in the sense of 'will it be better or worse'; what comes next will for sure be something else, completely, the Wholly Other. What comes next is irrelevant, because it leads away from the death experience and saps it of its effect.

This effect is all that counts. How it comes and when it comes are questions secondary to why it comes. *From the evidence which the psyche produces out of itself, the effect of the death experience is to bring home at a critical moment a radical transformation.* To step in at this moment with prevention in the name of life's preservation would frustrate the radical transformation. A thorough crisis is a death experience; we cannot have the one without the other. From this we are led to conclude that the experience of death is requisite for psychic life. This implies that the suicidal crisis, because it is one of the ways of experiencing death, must also be considered necessary to the life of the soul.

CHAPTER V

MEETING THE SUICIDE RISK

THE experience of death is necessary, but is actual suicide also necessary? How does the analyst proceed when the death experience is carried by suicide fantasies? How can he meet the needs of his analysand and keep separate inner and outer necessities?

Keeping distinct inner and outer is a major task of an analyst. If he uses his tools well he frees life from entangling projections and frees the soul from its worldliness. Inner and outer are kept apart so that later they may be re-united appropriately, the soul expressing itself in the world, and outer life feeding the inner man. *The suicide threat*, like any of the problems which bring a person into analysis in the first place, *is a confusion of inner and outer*. We suffer when we muddle psychic reality with concrete people and events, thus symbolising life and distorting its reality. And the reverse: we suffer when we are able to experience psychic reality only by acting out concretely our fantasies and ideas.

Outside and inside, life and soul, appear as parallels in 'case history' and 'soul history'. A case history is a biography of historical events in which one took part: family, school, work, illness, war, love. The soul history often neglects entirely some or many of these events, and spontaneously invents fictions and 'inscapes' without major outer correlations. The biography of the soul concerns experience. It seems not to follow the one-way direction of the flow of time, and it is reported best by emotions, dreams, and fantasies. Gulfs of years and events are dispensed with out of hand, while the dreams circle around and around certain aspects of the case history as symbols of meaning that carry the experience of the soul. These experiences owe their existence to the natural symbol-forming activity of the psyche. The experiences arising from major dreams, crises, and insights give definition to the personality. They too have 'names' and 'dates' like the outer events of case history; they are like boundary-stones which mark out one's own individual ground. These marks can be less denied than can the outer facts of life, for nationality, marriage, religion, occupation, and even one's own name can all be altered. To deny or try to erase one's own symbolic 'passport' is to betray one's own nature, and to then be lost in a rootless anonymity equal to, if not worse than, an outer disaster. Nor will any amount of reductive analysis be able to empty the meaning from these symbols by referring them to outer traumata.

Case history reports on the achievements and failures of life with the world of facts. But the soul has neither achieved nor failed in the same way because the soul has not worked in the same way. Its material is experience and its realisations are accomplished not just by efforts of will. The soul imagines and plays—and play is not chronicled by report. What remains of the years of our childhood play that could be set down in a case history? Children, and so-called 'primitive peoples', have no history; they have instead the residue of their play crystallised in myth and symbol, language and art, and in a style of life. Taking a soul history means capturing emotions, fantasies, and images by entering the game and dreaming the myth along with the patient. *Taking a soul history means becoming part of the other person's fate.* Where a case history presents a sequence of facts leading to diagnosis, soul history shows rather a concentric helter-skelter pointing always beyond itself. Its facts are symbols and paradoxes. Taking a soul history calls for the intuitive insight of the old-fashioned diagnostician and an imaginative understanding of a life-style which cannot be replaced by data accumulation and explanation through case history. We cannot get a soul history through a case history. But we can get a case history by prolonged exploration in soul history, which is nothing other than analysis itself.

As an analysis proceeds, it moves inward from the case history towards the soul history, that is, it explores complexes more for their archetypal meanings and less for their traumatic history. Soul history is recaptured by separating it from obfuscations in case history. The immediate family, for instance, become the real people they are, undistorted by inner meanings which they had been forced to carry. The rediscovery of soul history shows itself in the reawakening of emotion, fantasy, and dream, in a sense of mythological destiny penetrated by the transpersonal, and by spontaneous acausal time. It reflects the 'cure' from a chronic identification of the soul with outer events, places, and people. As this separation occurs, one is no longer a case but a person. Soul history emerges as one sheds case history, or, in other words, as one dies to the world as an arena of projection. Soul history is a living obituary, recording life from the point of view of death, giving the uniqueness of a person *sub specie aeternitatis*. As one builds one's death, so one writes one's own obituary in one's soul history.

The fact that there is soul history obliges us to consider the death of someone in analysis from this point of view. Case history classifies death by car crash differently from death by overdose of sleeping tablets. Death from disease, from accident, and from suicide are called different kinds of death—and so they are, from the outside. Even the more sophisticated classifications (unmeditated,

79

premeditated, and submeditated death) fail to give full credit to the involvement of the psyche in every death. These categories do not fully recognise that the soul is always meditating death. In Freud's sense, thanatos is ever-present; the soul needs death and death resides in the soul permanently.

Is an analyst less implicated in one kind of death than another? Is he more responsible in premeditated suicide than in submeditated accident or unmeditated cancer? His decision about a death—no matter how it be entered —depends upon his grasp of the soul history. His questions try to place this death in relation to the fundamental symbols, those markers of fate, given in the soul history. His responsibility is to the psychological fitness of events, to their inner justice or system, no matter how they appear outwardly.

From this perspective, the assassin's bullet, accidental and unmeditated for the victim, may belong within a mythic pattern of his fate, as much as a deliberate and meditated suicide after years of failed attempts. For it is not only that which belongs to the personal psychodynamics of a case history and is explicable through systems of motivations, that can be considered the right or necessary death. There are deaths that are wrong, like that of the hero, of the helpful companion, of the soul's love image, of the Man on that cross, which are yet tragically right. They fit within a definite mythic pattern. Myths have place for what is wrong and yet necessary.

Myths govern our lives. They steer a case history from below through the soul history. The irrationality, absurdity and horror of nature's experiments which we try to live are taken up by the images and motives of myth and in some way made understandable. Some people must live life wrongly and then leave it wrongly. How else can we account for crime, perversity, or evil? The fascinating intensity of such lives and deaths shows things at work beyond the merely human. Myth, which gives full place to every sort of atrocity, offers more objectivity to the study of such lives and deaths than any examination of personal motivation.

An analyst certainly does not have privileged access to nature's secrets. He is not able to read the ciphers and give oracular justifications. He can, however, *deo concedente*, through his familiarity with the soul history and the mythologems exposed there try to get to the bottom of things, below questions of rationally explicable motives and moralisms of right and wrong. The rational morality of life itself has always been open to question; is it any different for death?

From the perspective of soul history, the secret league determines the responsibility of the analyst (as we shall describe him in the latter part of this book). His responsibility extends as far as his involvement in, his participation with, the other person's soul history. Theoretically, he would participate equally in every kind of death, and *he would be no more responsible in suicide than in any other*. In suicide an analyst's failure of responsibility would mean not the bare act of suicide, as is thought when it is said that every suicide is a therapeutic failure. It would mean rather his failure to the secret league in two possible ways: either not being involved or not standing consciously for the involvement. The position of one foot in and one foot out must be held. Both feet out is non-involvement; both feet in is unconsciousness of the responsibility. *We are not responsible for one another's lives or deaths; each man's life and death is his own. But we are responsible to our involvements.* And John Donne's "And therefore never send to know for whom the bell tolls; it tolls for thee" becomes an ideal maxim for the analyst's attitude.

Because a case history always closes with death it cannot tell the whole story. It is time-bound. There is no follow-up. But the soul seems to have elements of premonition and transcendence. For the soul, it is as if death and even the manner and moment of entering it can be irrelevant, as if it did not matter, as if almost there were no death for the soul history at all.

Here begins the answer to the suicide question for the lay analyst. Here, too, the analytical parts with the medical viewpoint. The physician's point of view is bound to the fighting of death, to the prolonging of life, and to maintaining hope. The life of the body comes before all else, and therefore the medical reaction must be to save that life by prolonging it. The case history must be kept open as long as possible. The medical analyst is obliged by his training and tradition to give first consideration to organic death, which puts symbolic death and the death experience in second place. *But when the medical analyst gives more weight to the physical than to the psychological, he undermines his own analytical position.* He undervalues the soul as primary reality for analysis and takes his stand with the body. In other words, unless medical analysis abandons the medical framework, it cannot go the limit in an analysis. At the risk of life it is obliged to forsake the soul. It is no longer analytical psychotherapy, but medicine.

When an analyst puts concrete death first he does many unpsychological things. First, he has lost an individual stand and been overcome by the collective dread of death affecting him through the analysand. He thus has fed the other's anxiety and aided his repression of death. This contributes to the patient's neurosis. The honest attempt to confront whatever comes up is suddenly blocked. If an analyst prefers symbolic death to organic death because he feels the first is safe, he shows his patient that he has worked out an individual position about death in the psyche, but is still collective about death in the body. An early sign of succumbing to the collective dread of death is interrupting the individual consultations and turning the person over to a collective asylum. When the analyst does this he has set aside the psychological viewpoint, thereby losing contact with the soul of his patient. Yet loss of soul, not loss of life, should be his main dread. In addition, he has made an error of thinking by identifying the mode of an experience with the experience itself. He has failed to keep clear inner and outer.

We have elaborated the point that the soul needs the death experience. This can come about through various modes. Some of the inner images and emotions of the experience were mentioned in the preceding chapter. Suicide is but one of the modes; some others are: depression, collapse, trance, isolation, intoxication and exaltation, failure, psychosis, dissociation, amnesia, denial, pain and torture. These states can be experienced symbolically or concretely. They can be present in case history or soul history. *The mode to psychological experience seems not to matter to the soul providing it has the experience.* For some, organic death through actual suicide may be the only mode through which the death experience is possible.

This is the crux of the problem. Must, then, we guard against the death experience with medical measures because a suicide threat may bring physical death? Although the answer must always be individual, it is well to keep clear what the issue is. From the medical point of view, questions of the soul and its destiny are rather irrelevant when confronted with a corpse. No matter how committed an analyst might be to the soul, it would seem his work too is stopped by physical death. Treatment is over; the case is closed. There is no psychotherapy with a corpse. The medical argument finds medical measures always justified at the threat of suicide.

There is but one way of replying to a telling critique, and that is radically. Apart from the arguments showing the place of suicide in the death experience and the justification of suicide within a mythic pattern, we saw above that we do not know if the soul dies. We do not know if case history and soul history begin and end at the same moment, nor to what extent the first conditions the second. From the evidence of the soul itself, termination of case history is reflected in soul history in several ways: as irrelevant, as partial (only one aspect or image dies), as urgent challenge (to confront the salvation problem), or as rebirth with its attendant exalted emotions.

In non-western cultures, where the psyche is given more ear and where its 'treatment' forms a major part of every man's concerns, the souls of the dead are taken regularly into account and their lot fully considered, with prayer, with ancestor worship, with ritual observation, and through soul-mates, name-sakes, offspring, and friends. Communication with the dead continues. Our souls affect them. What we do with our souls has influence upon the progress of theirs. Their souls are still in process. We encounter them as revenants, in dreams, and through our own living images of them, living especially in those who were most involved in their soul history. If we follow radically the position of immortality, rather than fawn upon it with wishings, the analytical dialectic with the living image of the dead does not cease with physical death. We are still involved, and responsible. This view does not require ouija boards and poltergeists. It is not mysticism, but psychological realism. It is an induction from the empiricism of the soul's imagery and beliefs, evidenced in the practices and attitudes of peoples of most cultures. It is the basis of prayers

84

for the dead even in our own society, indicating that our relation with them is not over and how we treat them matters. It implies that treatment is never over; that analysis is truly interminable. In this sense, the corpse does not exclude psychotherapy; or better, analysis is anyhow not a dialectic with the body as body, either living or dead. The argument that there must be bodies for psychological relationship, if only for talking, can also be met. The dead other goes on existing as a psychological reality with whom one communicates, as exampled by the relations to dead saints and masters and the dead beloved. It is a comfortable rationalism, a psychologism, to claim that these psychic realities are only internal images or only objectifications of one's subjectivity. If psychic reality is reality, then we must follow its logic remorselessly. We cannot have it both ways: on the one hand, believed in as a kind of objective reality, and on the other, reduced to subjective figures and functions somewhere in the head. Physical reality drastically modifies psychic reality, and vice versa. But they do not coincide, except in those who have not been able to distinguish between their own soul and body. When a soul history begins to emerge from its confusion in bodily life—one sign of which is the death experience—then the independent reality of the soul and its transcendence of the body begin also to be realised. Then keeping a body alive is no longer the *sine qua non* for keeping alive every psychological relationship.

However, an analyst can go along with the medical view on one condition: that these medical measures are not against the soul: *Primum ANIMAE nihil nocere.* Treatment must be addressed to the soul, respect its emotions and imagery, and consider its claims. This means that the medical measures are not just emergency actions to prolong life, so that later on, psychotherapy can begin again. No, they are initiated primarily for the sake of the soul and form an adjunct to the psychotherapy. In other words, medical assistance is welcomed; medical substitution refused. The analytical viewpoint prevails. Where an analyst calls for medical intervention (drugs or confinement) *for medical reasons of prevention*, he has failed his calling. Practically, medical assistance means for an analyst that he be trusted by a physician who can accept the analyst's authority coming from his unique position 'inside' the situation. At this moment the physician is, in a sense, 'lay'.

As an analyst may not fall back on medical prevention, so also he may not try to 'symbolise' his way out. For the symbolic mode, if used defensively to prevent suicide, can cheat the person by a substitution that does not meet his need for the death experience. Then symbolisation will not work; the problem will either arise again—or can never.

The experience is necessary and there is no way out, neither medical nor symbolic. The thick walls thrown up against death attest to its power and our need. As much as worship, as much as love, as much as sex, hunger, self-preservation, and dread itself, is the urge towards the fundamental truth of life. If some call this truth God, then the impulse towards death is also towards the meeting with God, which some theologies hold is possible only by death. Suicide, taboo in theology, demands that God reveal Himself. And the God suicide demands, as well as the demon which would seem to prompt the act, is the *Deus absconditus* who is unable to be known, yet able to be experienced, who is unrevealed, yet more real and present in the darkness of suicide than the revealed God and all His testimony. Suicide offers immersion in, and possible regeneration through, the dark side of God. It would confront the last, or worst, truth in God, His own hidden negativity.

86

But all knowledge and argument will be of no use to the analyst in reasoning with the other person. The analyst may be convinced himself that the suicide fantasies are approaches to the death experience and that the patient is tragically muddling the symbolic and the concrete, but he will be unable to bring this over to the person in the other chair. Such arguments, if intellectual substitution, fail utterly to penetrate the crucial experience. They are thrown off by the whirring dynamism of the suicide emotion, falling blunted at the analyst's feet. Nor can one offer consolations of religion and philosophy. As Ringel points out, the intensity of the suicide impulse so grips the soul that whatever ideas are fed into the system will be converted into just that much more energy for the suicide fantasies. We do not have before us a 'logical fallacy', but a man in the grip of a symbol. The soul insists blindly and passionately on its intention. It will not be dissuaded; it will have its death—really, actually, now.

It must have its death, if it would be reborn. If death is deprived in any way of its overwhelming reality the transformation is misbegotten and the rebirth will be abortive.

The analyst cannot deny this need to die. He will have to go with it. His job is to help the soul on its way. He dare not resist the urge in the name of prevention, because *resistance only makes the urge more compelling and concrete death more fascinating.* Nor can he condemn every wish for suicide as an 'acting out', because again he sets up a prevention ban before he can be sure whether the act is necessary for the experience. He may not favour one mode over another. But by going with it, by being the bridge through whom the patient can enter death, *the experience may come before the actual death occurs.* This is not a symbolic substitution, although at that moment the symbolic mode may spontaneously appear. If it is born, it heralds the coming of the twice-born man. The symbolic mode means that a new kind of reality is coming into being. The person obsessed with suicide fantasies has not been able to experience death psychologically. He cannot experience *the reality of the psyche* apart from its projections, and therefore concrete reality and physical death are so compelling. But when the urge to physical death itself has been conquered by its realisation within the psyche, psychic reality takes on a numinous and indestructible quality. This is what tradition called the 'diamond body', more firm than life itself.

By going with the suicidal urge, an analyst begins to constellate the soul to present its requirements in a psychological form. He gives it first place and shies away from none of its intentions. Here, he has learned from the Shaman who places first importance upon the experience of death. He overcomes as far as possible prejudice against it in any form. Like the Shaman, he has already been to death himself; for the dead can best communicate with the dead. Like the Shaman, he welcomes the arrival of the urge as a sign of transformation, and he stands ready to help the other's entrance to the experience. He gives no especial weight to the physical mode of death, but *concentrates upon the experiences*. By confirming the psychic death, it can be released from its organic fixation.

This experience, as we have said, takes on many forms, such as rage, self-hatred, and torment, but principally it is despair. The more the impulse towards suicide is conscious, the more it will tend to colour all psychic life with despair. And the more this despair can be held, the less the suicide will 'just happen'. To hope for nothing, to expect nothing, to demand nothing. This is analytical despair. To entertain no false hopes, not even that hope for relief which brings one into analysis in the first place. This is an emptiness of soul and will. It is the condition present from that hour when, for the first time, the patient feels there is no hope at all for getting better, or even for changing, whatsoever. An analysis leads up to this moment and by constellating this despair lets free the suicidal impulse. Upon this moment of truth the whole work depends, because this is the dying away from the false life and wrong hopes out of which the complaint has come. As it is the moment of truth, it is also the moment of despair, because there is no hope.

Where the analyst can put aside his medical reaction to offer hope through treatment, he can enter the despair with the patient. By yielding his own hope, he can begin to accept the patient's experience that there is nothing to be done. So, *he offers nothing but the experience itself.* We cannot go beyond this despair by resuscitating drowned hopes, injecting suggestions and advice, or prescribing remedies. If the despair is thorough, presenting the clinical signs of depression, suicidal fantasies tend to become the major content of the hours. Yet the situation is not more precarious than when these same contents were lurking in the depths and the analysand was clinging to chimeras in a sea of confusion.

To himself, the analyst might reflect that offering nothing is actually the best form of treatment because it affords the natural movement of the psyche a chance to express itself. Should he act on this idea, he is not offering nothing; he is again treating. He has left the analysand alone in the despair and betrayed him again by substituting. This substitution is more subtle: it offers a mock despair which is really a hopeful prevention.

At this point an analyst is forced to find out why he wants the other person to live. If his patient means only a charge, a burden assumed by 'taking on the case', he will be unconsciously killing his patient, because somewhere we all want to be rid of burdens. The sense of being a burden is already so strong in many who commit suicide, that often the act is done altruistically, to lighten the load for others. When the chips are down, such principles as therapeutic commitment and responsibility to life are not enough. The analyst is cornered into his personal eros, into feeling why this individual is personally valuable to him. Do I truly need him and want him to live? What is the uniqueness of our relationship? How am I involved with this person as with no one else? Without this personal involvement, each patient could be any other patient. All talk of individuality would be empty.

Without this personal eros, there is no vessel to contain the destructive forces, the desires to hurt and kill, which can be constellated during the crisis. The close bond focuses the suicidal affects in the analysis. The rage, hatred, and despair seem directed against the analyst, personally. Some interpreters have tried reducing the whole matter to transference enactions of childhood struggles. True, a taint of childhood stains most of our actions, especially during crises; but the attack on the analyst is better considered in the light of the secret league and the ambivalence constellated by the symbolic nature of every close personal tie. The main purpose that these destructive affects try to achieve is: to dissolve the vessel of relationship itself into despair. Therefore, there must be room even for despair within an analyst's eros. His eros will then not be used as a method, as 'live because I love you', to coerce the patient out of despair.

By staying true to the hopeless condition as it is, he constellates a kind of stoic courage in himself and the other person. By keeping this vigil, the threat of panic action recedes. They stand still together looking at life and death —or life *or* death. There is no treatment going on because both have given up hope, expectations, demands. They have left the world and its outside viewpoint, taking as the only reality the images, emotions, and meanings which the psyche presents. Death has already entered because the rage to live has passed. The case history records 'nothing happening', while the soul history may be realising a profound and wordless experience.

Keeping this watch also means paying attention to the *absurd and trivial details of life.* For the death experience is not only grand, profound, and wordless; it also dissolves the daily into nonsense. All sorts of things happen; miracles and mistakes together. But this careful consideration of detail may not be used with therapeutic intentions: to 'help life to go on', or for 'ego support'. The focus on absurdity seems a spontaneous part of the death experience itself, bringing out wholly new and astonishing meanings from old habits. And the transformation is marked by an awareness of paradox and synchronicity where sense and nonsense merge.

Some say they stay alive only because of their children, their parents—others. With this in mind the analyst may begin to remind the patient of the effect of this death on others. But here again this avoids the risk in its naked intensity. Suicide puts society, human responsibility, and even the community of souls *in extremis.* For this reason, as we have seen, the official points of view condemn it with good reason. *Suicide is the paradigm of our independence from everyone else.* It must be that way during the suicide crisis because at this moment everyone else stands for the *status quo,* for life and the world which must be absolutely denied. These things no longer really count. Reminder of them serves only to intensify the drive. Therefore, an analyst can well take the suicide gesture as a 'cry for help',—but not to live. Rather it is a cry for help to die, to go through the death experience with meaning. The analyst is effective as a link with life only when he does not assert this link. He stands neither

91

for life nor death, but for the experience of these opposites.

As paradigm of independence, suicide is also selfishness. The world shrinks to the small measure of 'me': my action, my death. Abnegation is simply omnipotence in disguise. Whether in stealthy silence or in full-view from the downtown ledge, there is a selfish obsession with my own importance. And the world of others—as the emergency wards where those failing their attempts are first brought—reacts with contempt for this selfishness. However, an analyst can yet see within this selfishness the small seed of selfhood. A seed must be closed in on itself in order to generate its own being; it must be exclusively 'me'. In the negative selfishness is an affirmation of individuality.

The analyst continues the analytical process by fixing in consciousness the experiences as they unfold. They become consciously realised in the personality through confirmation and amplification. The death experience is not merely passed through. It is achieved, accomplished, and built into the psyche.

By preventing nowhere, he makes possible the patient's experience of death. *He gives the person the opportunity denied him everywhere.* The analyst now plays the true psychopompos, guider of souls, by not breaking the bond of trust at the moment when it is most crucial. He has kept his faith with the secret league. The person knows he can rely on the analyst, because the understanding between them cannot be broken even by death. By preventing nowhere, the analyst is nevertheless doing the most that can be done to prevent the actual death. By his having entered the other's position so fully, the other is no longer isolated. He, too, is no longer able to break freely the secret league and take a step alone.

Analytical despair is nothing else than facing reality together, and the *a priori* of all human reality is death. The individual is thus encouraged to meet his overpowering need for the transcendent and absolute. We are back to Spinoza's proposition that the liberated man thinks of death but his meditation is of life.

Transformation begins at this point where there is no hope. Despair produces the cry for salvation, for which hope would be too optimistic, too confident. It was not with a voice of hope that Jesus called, "*Eli, Eli, lama sabachthani?*" The cry on the cross is the archetype of every cry for help. It sounds the anguish of betrayal, sacrifice, and loneliness. Nothing is left, not even God. My only certainty is my suffering which I ask to be taken from me by dying. An animal awareness of suffering, and full identification with it, becomes the humiliating ground of transformation. Despair ushers in the death experience and is at the same time the requirement for resurrection. Life as it was before, the *status quo ante*, died when despair was born. There is only the moment as it is—the seed of whatever might come—if one can wait. The waiting is all and the waiting is together.

This emphasis on experience, this loyalty to the soul and the dispassionate scientific objectivity towards its phenomena, and this affirmation of the analytical relationship may release the transformation the soul has been seeking. It may come only at the last minute. It may never come at all. But there is no other way.

If it does not come, the analyst is left alone to judge whether the suicide was necessary or not. Necessary means unavoidable, like accident or disease. Plato's famous criterion for justified suicide was stated in the *Phaedo* 62, where he has Socrates say: ". . . there may be reason in saying that a man should wait, and not take his own life until God summons him . . ." Hitherto, this "summons" (variously translated as "necessity", "compulsion")

93

was always taken as an outer event, something which comes as a dire circumstance (defeat, accident, disease, catastrophe). However, could not the necessity also be from the soul? If an analyst has permitted the death experience *to the utmost* and still the soul insists on organic death through suicide, cannot this too be considered an unavoidable necessity, a summons from God?

To pass beyond this point by speculating why some must enter death in this manner, why God summons some to suicide, means raising questions about God and what He wants with man. However, this would lead us onto the terrain of metaphysics and theology, that is, beyond the borders of psychology and this book.

Part Two

THE CHALLENGE OF ANALYSIS

"I can hardly draw a veil over the fact that we psychotherapists ought really to be philosophers or philosophic doctors—or rather that we already are so . . ."

(C. G. Jung: Psychotherapy and a Philosophy of Life, 1942)

"Method in psychology acquires an importance that far exceeds that which it possesses in the other disciplines. For it is both a means of becoming, as well as a means of discovery . . . Verification in psychology therefore demands that every step forward, every hypothesis that is checked and confirmed, should also satisfy the values of the soul and hence be itself a means towards their realisation. Thus what a psychologist comes to know about the soul qualifies him in a way that scientific knowledge can never qualify the scientist. For the scientist it is always possible, indeed it is imperative that he should divorce his personality from what he knows and from the matter to which this knowledge applies: the application of his method is independent of its effects on him and his investigations are carried on in spite of rather than through his personality. Not so the psychologist who, at the same time as he studies his world, is creating it as well as creating himself."

(Evangelos Christou: The Logos of the Soul, 1963)

"I am not a mechanism, an assembly of various sections.
And it is not because the mechanism is working wrongly,
　　　　that I am ill.
I am ill because of wounds to the soul, to the deep
　　　　emotional self
and the wounds to the soul take a long, long time, only
　　　　time can help
and patience, and a certain difficult repentance
long, difficult repentance, realisation of life's mistake, and
　　　　the freeing oneself
from the endless repetition of the mistake
which mankind at large has chosen to sanctify."

(D. H. Lawrence: Healing)

CHAPTER VI

MEDICINE, ANALYSIS, AND THE SOUL

OUR discussion of suicide has shown how an analyst views his work. By taking up the most difficult of all analytical problems, the challenges of analysis have been focused most pointedly. These challenges and the response which the analyst has had to develop out of his own experience lead inevitably to formulating an *ontology of analysis*. This implies that the time has come in psychotherapy for working out the archetypal root of the discipline. When this has been done, the term 'lay analysis' will fall away because the analyst will no longer be considered, nor consider himself, from alien points of view. He will no longer be lay priest, lay physician, lay psychologist. He will have his own ground, surveyed and mapped in all contours.

Beginnings have already been made from various directions to delimit the field of analysis. Existential psychiatry is attempting to recast psychotherapy in a new mould. The investigations of communication and semantics, of the therapeutic transaction, of transference and countertransference, as well as the current cross-fertilisations between religion and psychotherapy, are all approaches to new descriptions of psychotherapy and attempts to demarcate it from neighbouring territory.

A thorough effort, a true ontology of psychotherapy, will depend upon a *science of the soul*. This science would delimit the nature of psychic reality *per se*, as distinct from mental contents, acts of behaviour, attitudes, etc. It would take up the problems of method and of verification and falsifiability of hypotheses. It would work out criteria for recognising psychic reality and set down what it means by psychological truth and what are psychological facts. It would also have to clarify those fundamental experiences of analysis: insight, meaning, regression, transference, neurosis—and 'experience' itself. This would lead to an ontology of the 'inner' which still is inadequately conceived as inside the body or the head because of the language and perspectives borrowed from other fields.

This is a large programme, and one well beyond the ambition of this book. It requires radical new thinking, thinking which willingly leaves the ground of physical science, of theology, of academic psychology, of medicine, in short, of every area but its own. This task may begin by separating what is psyche *per se* from the various fields where it shows itself. Since everything human can be said to reflect the psyche in some facet, the separation of the soul by laying bare its structure, contents, and functions is a task that can be done only after one has refused the tools and vessels from other fields. This refusal is a pressing necessity, as the enquiry into suicide has shown. All other fields view the problems of the soul from outside angles. Analysis, alone, starts from the individual person. It is therefore the first tool to be used in building a science of the soul. Because it is the proper instrument, the conclusions analysis has already established—no matter how fragmentary and paradoxical—must be given more weight than those from other areas.

The ontology of analysis cannot be laid down by equating analysis with existence and by borrowing from existential philosophy a foreign language and a foreign system of weights and measures. The ontology of analysis, for all its similarities to philosophy, is an *analytical psychology*. It is a psychological analysis, an analysis of the psyche—and not a phenomenological or existential philosophising. An analytical psychology is primarily a science of unconscious processes. These processes are like creeks and streams forming the network of that major river system, the individuation process, flowing through each human and prospectively shaping him into himself on its journey towards the sea. The various unconscious processes can also be understood as mythologems, or mythic fragments, appearing in behaviour and dream which together make up the central myth of each person's individual process. Analysis aims at encouraging the flow and connecting the symbolic fragments into a mythic pattern. In studying these processes, we find system, law, order, and coherence. It is not merely a bland acceptance of whatever exists as in *daseinanalyse*. The *dasein* of individuality has neither pattern nor prospect. Anything goes; because the criteria for authentic existence cannot be created out of one individual's consciousness alone. Subjectivity is not balanced by the objective psyche. This leads to a worship of individuality in its existential loneliness instead of reverence for those fundamental unconscious processes which are at the same time universally human and the ground of individuation.

For this science of unconscious processes, a vast body of knowledge is required which can be described and communicated objectively and used for clinical prediction. The investigation of these processes requires research in an attitude of scientific enquiry. The ontology therefore must be worked out in connection with empirical facts. This is not the method of existential ontology, which gives little heed to empirical facts, to scientific investigation, to the unconscious, to the description of psychological processes, or even to psychology itself, which has become for it but an inadequate handmaiden of existential philosophy.

The most important contribution towards clarifying

psychic reality has been made by Jung, who uncovered the fundamental dynamic patterns of the psyche which he called archetypes, or organs of the soul. In staking his claim for psychic reality as an objective field having its own laws and requiring its own methods, he ran into opposition from the orthodoxies of medicine, theology, and academic psychology. They too claim rights to the psyche. Psychotherapy began within the terrain of medicine, and theology considers one of its provinces to be the human soul. Jung seemed to be carving the ground from under their feet by describing psychic processes and contents which they had already mapped and named. For them, the analyst was invading their precincts and was nothing else but lay.

Jung had the courage to hold his ground. He stood for the soul as the first human reality. He took no root metaphor from biology or sociology with its emphasis on species or group, but, by demonstrating the capacity for self-transformation of the human personality towards uniqueness, he stood squarely for the individual. He gave credit to his patients; he believed their souls. By having the courage to stand for one's own experience, one begins to give real being to the soul, thereby furthering the ontology which is not yet built. This is the only way that it can be built. *It depends upon each individual involved in analysis to stand for his experience*—his symptoms, suffering, and neurosis, as well as the invisible, positive accomplishments—in the face of a world that gives these things no credit. The soul can become a reality again only when each of us has the courage to take it as the first reality in our own lives, to stand for it and not just 'believe' in it.

To build an ontology of psychology we need not wait for a synthesising genius to construct a unified system in which all practitioners can find their cells. This eclectic approach has been tried for years, yielding only new schools and new arguments. Psychological ontology is being built by analysts existentially within themselves, by each of us standing his own ground, by being where he is, by being in the analytical process. 'Being in the process', as some Jungians are wont to call their experience of analysis, is a phrase that describes a special state of being and therefore an ontological position. It can be compared with those states of 'being in it' of the painter or writer and 'being in love'. 'Being in analysis' for an analysand carries that sort of meaning. He experiences himself fundamentally—ontologically—separated from others who are not in analysis just as 'being in love' removes lovers from the normal. To get to this position, we need not take an ontological leap towards a new kind of being, but only stand for our individual experiential differences, those glimmerings of uniqueness.

Before the work of Jung can be carried further by analysts—and they must do the job, since their thinking will always be closest to the facts of experience—analysts will have to free themselves from those remains of theology, of academic psychology, and especially of medicine which still clutter the ground and which are false markers for an analytical psychology. One such remain is the term 'lay analysis' itself which this work is attempting to expose. *This work also attempts to clear the ground by contesting every inch of the claims of theology, of academic psychology, and of medicine over analysis.* It is not so much to attack as it is to liberate occupied territory, so that the ontology for psychotherapy can one day be built on its own ground. Our campaign is for analysis, the viewpoint of the analyst, and the root metaphor of the soul from which this viewpoint arises. Only where the viewpoint is obstructed by remnants of old outlooks—especially medical, psychiatric, Freudian—is it necessary to tear down.

Old oppositions of science versus religion, as in the days of Shaw, or the later one of two cultures, as in the days of Snow, are no longer the real oppositions. The new opposition, the real one in this generation, is between the soul and all that would butcher or purchase it, between analysis and every official position of medicine, theology, and academic psychology that would encroach upon it, between the analyst and everyone else. Suicide is the issue for laying this conflict bare.

There is no use taking up any of the usual positions today. We are all so sick and have been so long on the edge of mass suicide and are groping so for personal solutions to vast collective problems, that today, if ever, anything goes. The fences are down: medicine is no longer the preserve of the physician, death for the aged, and theology for the ordained.

Of course, the physician himself has a soul, and as healer among the suffering he is faced with it as perhaps no one. But modern medicine excludes the soul from its teachings, requiring the physician to act as if he had none and as if the patient were primarily body. Modern medicine splits the physician off from his own soul. He may believe in it and follow it in his own life, while going about in his profession as if it did not exist. He is cut off from his authentic roots in Asklepian medicine, and the issue between medicine and analysis is but a restatement of the conflict between Hippocratic and Asklepian healing. Medical training today so warps the student against the psychological background of medicine that all virtues of the Hippocratic approach are outweighed by its one-sided disadvantages. Because the physician so stands for one side, the analyst is driven to another extreme. This unfortunate fact constellates the medical position even more forcefully in the analyst's own unconscious, so that at times he no longer knows from where the distortion arises: modern medicine and its advocates or his own medical shadow and the nineteenth-century background of analysis. Just as non-medical analysis falls under the shadow of medicine, as lay, so does medicine catch the shadow projections of analysis.

This hardly leads to balanced discussion. But this is perhaps just as well, since balance keeps one away from the edge. And it is to the edge one has to go for the enquiry into suicide. It is the edge, with the abyss just behind one's back, that evokes the *cri de cœur* cutting through every balanced presentation. What has been done to the soul by its shepherds and its physicians in the name of 'mental health', 'suicide prevention', 'dynamic psychotherapy', 'pastoral counselling', and 'research studies' requires an answer in kind, and this cannot be balanced.

Analysis belongs to analysts; only what they think about their work is valid, and only their criteria for psychotherapy and for training are to be accepted. All others—physicians, clergy, psychiatrists, academic psychologists, existential philosophers, sociologists—are lay, until they have left the old positions of their alien professions and stand for the soul first. Unfortunately, because so many analysts still prefer the accepted style of the old structures from which they have come, they build their new academies in the same way. They continue with their medical ideas and their descriptions based on the natural sciences, materialism, and causality. Or, they abandon the scientific spirit altogether in sudden vogues of Existentialism from Germany or Zen from Japan.

Our first task therefore is to speak to analysts about analysis, to point out where analysts can and do differ from medicine, in fact, where they no longer practise, think, or feel like their medical contemporaries, even though they are akin in many ways to the traditional notion of the physician. As we go along from chapter to chapter, we shall be contrasting a medical and an analytical point of view, aiming above all to show how important it is that the practice of psychotherapy leave behind its medical background and set out on its own.

The first to recognise that medicine was neither the sufficient nor necessary background for the practice of analysis was Freud. In a sense, then, our concern with separating medicine from analysis in this second part of the book is a continuation of his essay, *The Question of Lay Analysis*.

Freud saw soon enough that medicine had to be partly abandoned. He said that in psychotherapy "the ill were not like other ill persons, the lay practitioner not really lay, and the physicians not what one might expect from physicians". The analyst does not physically examine his patients; physical treatments are not used; for organic ailments the patient is referred; medical equipment is absent from the consulting room; there is neither white coat nor black bag. What kind of a 'Doctor' is this who is not interested in medicine, in etiology and diagnosis, in prescription, nor even in relief or cure?

A generation has passed since Freud's arguments and the heated discussions on lay analysis in the 1920s. The change in the kinds of patients from then to now has added more support to Freud's position. Today, the analyst sees more 'personality disorders' who come for 'character analysis' than those coming for symptom relief. Analysis has moved even farther away from the medical therapy of symptoms and closer to the psychology of the whole individual.

Giving up the medical methods of the consulting room abandons only minor outposts; the main medical position has been kept. It continues to guide other techniques in the same medical way, tending to give analysis a pathological bias towards things of the soul. The danger to analysis from medicine comes less from medicine's weakness than from its strength, i.e., its coherently rational materialism. The knowledge learned in medical school, most of which Freud found so useless for analysis, is also less the problem (since academic learning in every field requires an accumulation of irrelevancies) than is the model of medical thinking, its *weltanschauung*. Freud strongly favoured lay analysts, and in a letter barely a year before his death he reaffirmed his arguments: ". . . I insist on them even more intensely than before, in the face of the obvious American tendency to turn psychoanalysis into a mere house-maid of psychiatry" (Jones, p. 323).

Nevertheless, Freudian therapy still presents in general the medical point of view. Freud's fears have been realised: Freudian analysis has become the hand-maid of psychiatry. The modern eclectic psycho-dynamic approach of the usual psychiatrist is the watered-down spirit of Freud. It is a popular spirit that can be held without danger in any vessel of common clay. Thus the usual psychiatrist is spared the efforts of refining his personality in the distilling retort of a deep analysis, beyond a short catharsis to clean out his unconscious while in psychiatric residency.

The main lot of Freud's followers have rejected his positions both on lay analysis and on the death drive, which shows that Freudian therapy remains a medical discipline. By denying Freud's position on these crucial issues, Freudian therapy becomes medically acceptable. Freudians must indeed go against their master with their continued emphasis upon a medical degree for analytical training, since the root metaphor which informs their attitudes does not differ from that of medicine.

Is it necessary to retain medical thinking in order to

be scientific, to be empirical? Science is an attitude of mind, requiring reflection, conscientious honesty, and an ordered, living interplay between fact and idea. Analysts can still be scientists in the basic sense of the word—and empirical scientists—without recourse to medicine. Jung at times missed this point. When under fire for 'unscientific speculation', he retreated to the posture of 'medical psychologist'. 'Medical' for him at these times meant 'empirical'. He had developed his ideas in keeping with the empirical facts that presented themselves in his practice. But one need not be medical to keep in touch with the facts appearing in the consulting room, or to be concerned with the welfare of one's charges.

Had Freud pressed further with the question of lay analysis, he would have been led to withdraw from the medical position altogether and not have been content just to show that medical training was unnecessary and insufficient for analysis. *If medical training does not fulfil the conditions for analysis, then analysis must be something different from medicine.* It is doubtful that Freud could have gone to the end with this line of thought, because he was no longer a young man and he was still hemmed in by his own nineteenth-century medical mind. (His teachers, after all, were born in the first part of the last century.) Going to the end of this line of thought and going to the end in psychotherapy leads into questions of death. Here, too, Freud retained a view bound closely to the natural sciences, shown by his principle of Thanatos, a death-drive opposed to life. This principle for Freudians carries so many of the negative sides of human nature that when Freud says "the goal of life is death", it is the pessimistic statement of a natural scientist who is led by the network of his system to fight death in the name of life. The fundamental basis of the medical approach to analysis will always be pessimistic, since, no matter what we do, life is eventually conquered by death, and physical reality is always primary to psychic reality.

But the statement need not be pessimistic. Going to the end in analysis means seeing "the goal of life is death" in an altogether different way. It means taking this proposition as the logical ground for an ontology of analysis. Going to the end in analysis means going to death and starting from there. If death is life's goal, then death is more basic than life itself. If a choice must be made between the two, then life must yield to its goal. Physical reality which is limited to life only must yield primacy to psychic reality, since the reality of the soul includes both life and death. The paradox of the soul is that, in spite of its ancient definition as the vital principle, it is also always on the side of death. It is given with an opening to what is beyond life. It works at its perfection beyond questions of physical health and life. We meet this uncanny peculiarity of the soul in the images and emotions of every analysis, where the most important concerns of the soul involve death. The reality of the psyche would seem to draw us into an inexpressible and irrational absolute which we call 'death'. *The more real we take the soul to be, the more we grow concerned with death.* The soul's development is towards death and through death, calling for death experiences as we have seen. This *a priori* involvement of the soul with death has been called in philosophical and religious language the transcendence and immortality of the soul.

An analyst can therefore go to the end in psychotherapy when he stands for the reality of the psyche. He can meet the risk of suicide without fighting, without medical action. He can abandon the basis of medicine itself, the fight for physical life, because he has abandoned the ontological position of materialism and scientific naturalism which says that physical reality is the only reality. So now must go as well the attitudinal background of medicine against which the analyst's work has hitherto been judged and by which it has been oppressed and shadowed. Some of this background will occupy us in the following chapters.

CHAPTER VII

A MATTER OF WORDS

THE practice of analysis is not clearly divided between medical and lay. In the public mind practitioners of all sorts are identified with analysts: psychiatrists, social workers, group therapists, pastoral counsellors, healers, clinical psychologists, and many others. The public knows little about analysis and little about what sort of training is necessary for its practice. Those who have been to a psychiatrist or psychotherapist or psycho-analyst assume that all psychotherapy is more or less the same as the one, whatever the sort, that they have known.

The prime requisite for the practice of analysis has always been very simple. The analyst must be analysed himself before analysing others. This was the original premise of Freud and Jung and is maintained by the genuine Freudians and Jungians today. It is called a recognised training analysis and it includes as well study of the unconscious. How many hours of analysis an analyst has had, whether or not he has a doctor's degree, whether or not he be recognised by his colleagues, licensed by the state, or graduated from an analytical training institute, such questions are all secondary to the first criterion: *the analyst must have been analysed before he analyses others.* This is both the prime training and the test of the vocation. An analyst may therefore regard those who have not been analysed—no matter what their academic credentials and years of clinical experience—as lay. Naturally, he tends to favour those whose analysis has been long and thorough and with a recognised master, who have carried out control analyses under supervision, and who have graduated from a training institute.

The public tends to lump together all those who have to do with psychotherapy, usually missing the fact that *most psychiatrists have themselves never been analysed* and that analysis is not a required part of their training. Of course, many other psychiatrists because they have fulfilled analytical requirements are analysts as well as psychiatrists. Psychiatrists have been trained first in medicine, then in clinics with interned patients with whom for the large part physical methods of treatment are prescribed. Analysts, on the other hand, work with ambulatory patients and use psychological methods. Some psychiatrists move from the clinic into private practice on the basis of their experience with others only, without themselves having been through an analysis of their own. To an analyst, this kind of psychiatrist—if he does any analysis—is a lay analyst, even though he be a qualified physician and psychiatric specialist.

The same holds true for psychologists. A psychologist trained in the universities holding the degree of Doctor of Philosophy may or may not have been analysed, may or may not belong to a professionally recognised society of analysts. Some practise analysis on the basis of what they have learned for their degree requirements. This academic learning of such fields as statistical methods, processes of consciousness associated with the nervous system, laboratory experiments with animal behaviour, psychological testing and counselling in mental clinics, is relevant only for general psychology. Again, these psychologists remain lay if they analyse without the specific psychological training won from having been analysed.

The term 'lay analysis' is used also by analysts in another way. This is what used to be called by Freud "*wilde Analyse*". The analytical profession is organised into different local and international societies and follows different schools of thought. For all the differences, the analytical profession has certain requirements for admission. If someone has not had enough analysis, or he has not been with a recognised analyst, or if he fails to have the correct academic credentials for that society, or is not licensed because his credentials are foreign or not in those fields stipulated by law, etc., etc., and yet he practises analysis, then we have again a 'lay' analyst.

However, today, *the issue of lay analysis is presented chiefly from the point of view of medicine.* The very word 'lay' is pejorative, coming originally from the medical side. It divides analysis into two sorts: medical and non-medical. The strict medical argument runs as follows: Analysis is a specialisation of psychiatry and psychiatry is a specialisation of medicine; therefore, the analyst is a specialist physician. Analysis is a therapeutic treatment dealing with psychopathology. All such treatments belong wholly and only to the medical profession, who alone are authorised by themselves and by the law to carry on therapeutic treatment. Anyone who practises analysis is practising medicine; anyone practising medicine without a medical degree is not only lay, but quack.

This extreme position is not usually so boldly stated. Nevertheless, it needs to be stated, because it has such influence upon analysis. It affects the professional position of the non-medical analyst. At times, an analyst may have to work junior to a psychiatrist who has never been analysed nor studied the unconscious; or worse, he may be prohibited by law from practising his profession altogether.

Far more serious is the effect the medical position has had upon the thinking and practising of all analysts, medical and non-medical. The argument—analysis is a specialisation of psychiatry and psychiatry is a specialisation of medicine—subtly undermines the analyst from within through his own attitudes. He believes he is working within a medical discipline. Thus, he tends to conceive his problems and formulate his answers in a medical way, which leads him to regard himself as lay. He adopts the medical position without knowing it. He misses its specious reasoning, for it is analysis only that is altogether committed to the problems of the psyche. Its material, its methods, and its goals are all psychological. It is the only discipline which investigates the psyche in its natural setting, that is, within a relationship. *For analysis can be most simply defined as the study within a relationship of unconscious psychological events for the purpose of their conscious realisation.* Psychiatry is only one approach to these events, and this approach is limited by its medical basis. Until the analyst has cleared away within himself these inauthentic models of thinking, he will never be up to the task of building his discipline in his own fashion.

Moreover, until he stands wholly with the soul he will always fail his vocation and his analysand.

It has been argued that because analysis began within medicine it belongs there. Freud and Jung were physicians, the former a specialist in neurology, the latter in psychiatry. Analysis began in medicine and was discovered by physicians simply because they were the only ones to give ear to psychopathology, the suffering of the soul. After Darwin had dug out man's ape ancestors and Nietzsche had announced that God is dead, and after the rational materialism of the nineteenth century, the soul ran for succour into the consulting room of the alienist. The psyche had become alienated from the world about it, for this world had lost its soul. Freud listened to his hysterical patients, as Jung did to his schizophrenics. They found meaning, and thereby rediscovered the soul in a place it was least expected—among the sick and insane. Though found again there, it is questionable whether the soul and its sufferings must remain a province of medicine for ever.

In other words, those in quest find their search leads them eventually to an analyst. We can ridicule this vogue of 'seeing an analyst', but it remains a psychological fact. Religion and medicine, then and now, are too sane to offer anything effective to the soul *in extremis*, and it is *in extremis*, in the sufferings and symptoms rooted in the unconscious that we first begin to sense the soul. The soul has been buried there and it wants *psychological* help, help in its own language. A person asks for someone concerned with the psyche as such, a soul-specialist—not a physician or a priest, nor even a friend. Analysts did not ask to be priests nor physicians, and were there only more wise friends and true lovers! Analysis has been forced into its position because no one else would have anything to do with the psyche, *per se*. Analysis started off where the soul lay in darkness, and analysts thus became specialists in darkness. They stood for the unconscious and the repressed, and their work was of the left-hand, sinister, quack, unacademic, a devil's minion. But from this extreme position, the analyst could meet the soul which had also been exiled to life *in extremis*.

Originally, medicine had another approach. This is brought out by the basic meanings of the words for the physician. We shall see through an investigation of these words that, as medicine turned from the old approach and took up more and more the viewpoint of the natural sciences, the aspects left vacant have begun to be occupied by the analyst.

'Physician', like 'physics', comes from the Greek word for nature, *physis*. The stem of this word is *bhu*, which means to grow, to produce. From the same stem comes 'to be' and 'being'. The physician was originally the student of nature. He was a philosopher, concerned with the nature of being, or ontology, as well as with the being of nature. He learned about nature through his study of man, which was always the whole man, not just his nature conceived as his matter. This was before man and nature were split and before nature had become identified with matter. But since the seventeenth century, physics has taken over the philosophy of nature, and the physician turns to physics for his ultimate model of human nature and for his methods in handling it. By moving towards natural science, he has moved away from the nature of man. This has resulted in both the great achievements of modern medicine and the great difficulties of the modern physician in understanding that in his patients which cannot be explained by rational science.

'Doctor' comes from the Latin, *docere*, to teach. It is cognate to *ducere*, to lead, and to *educare*, educate. A 'docile' animal is easily instructed; a 'document' (*documentum*) is a lesson, just as a 'doctrine' (*doctrina*) is the content of a teaching, a science. The men who are called in Catholic tradition the 'Doctors of the Church' were the great theologians and philosophers. The only physicians entitled to the calling of Doctor in the medieval medical faculties were those who taught, as does the *Dozent* in the German language faculties today. The implication is that he who carries the title of doctor ought to be a man of learning, scholarship, and enquiry, with the ability to teach others. It is curious to find this title now so exclusive to the medical practitioner.

The words 'medicine' and 'medical' (*médecin* means physician in French) again come from Latin. *Medicus* is close to the Latin verb *mederi* = to care; and thus to 'medication', 'remedy'. Going deeper, we find again a philosophical aspect. *Mederi*, to care, is cognate with *medeteri*, meditation, reflection. They are rooted in the ancient Iranian *vi-mad*, to consider, appreciate, measure, which are all acts of reflective consciousness. Comparable is the Gaelic, *midiur*= judge; *med*= balance. As Prince and Layard point out, *med* as balance is the fulcrum or middle thing (*medius*) that holds the opposites together by dividing (*mediare*) them apart.

This can be interpreted to mean that the care and cure which medicine offers is linked with meditation, with deep reflective thought. 'Measure' and 'balance' go beyond their pharmaceutical usage. The *medicus* takes the measure of himself as well as he measures fever and dosage. He needs to be in consultation with himself in order to give adequate consultation to the patient. Care and remedy are more than events produced through external medication. Medication is, in fact, meditation requiring consciousness from the physician. The pondering of theory is as necessary as practice; consultations with one's self as fruitful as consultations with colleagues. Meditation is *theoria*, that contemplative and visionary activity of the religious life. In short, 'medicine' leads to self-analysis.

The Greek word *therapeia* refers also to care. The root is *dher*, which means carry, support, hold, and is related to *dharma*, the Sanskrit meaning 'habit' and 'custom' as 'carrier'. The therapist is one who carries and takes care as does a servant (Greek= *theraps, therapon*). He is also one to lean upon, hold on to, and be supported by, because *dher* is also at the root of *thronos*= throne, seat, chair. Here we strike an etymological root of the analytical relationship. The chair of the therapist is indeed a mighty throne constellating dependency and numinous projections. But the analysand also has his chair, and the analyst is both servant and supporter of the analysand. Both are emotionally involved and the dependence is mutual. However, this dependence is not personal, upon each other. Rather it is a dependence upon the objective psyche which both serve together in the therapeutic process. By carrying, by paying careful attention to and devotedly caring for the psyche, the analyst translates into life the meaning of the word 'psychotherapy'. The psychotherapist is literally the *attendant of the soul.*

It is worth noting that the word therapy has all but vanished from medical use. It turns up more in the non-medical professions: psychotherapy, group-therapy, physiotherapy, occupational therapy, play-therapy, etc. Here, emotional aspects, such as loving care and concern for each other, are primary; whereas in medicine they have been replaced by more intellectual procedures, such as diagnosis, pharmacology, and surgery.

Where the physician has moved away from this sense of therapy, he now is closer to the first Greek word for physician—*iatros.* The origin of *iatros* is dubious, but there is authoritative opinion saying that it means 'he who re-warms'; the *iatros* is the one who stirs up and re-animates, who fights cold death. *Iatros* is said to be akin to *ira*, the Latin concept of anger, aggression, the spirit of will, of power, temper, wrath, irascibility. *'Psychiatrist' thus would mean animator or inspirer of the psyche.* He brings back warmth and temper by stimulation and excitement. Electro-shock and other external stimuli are modern and concrete expressions of this ancient idea.

There are other ways to stir up, re-animate, and inspire. Vivification can come about also through emotional involvement with the patient in the therapeutic process. Here the physician has recourse to his own spirit and soul (anima) in order to bring warmth and life to the patient. Unfortunately, too often his white coat, his sterilised equipment, the medical atmosphere in general, prevent this emotional involvement. Unfortunately, too, the medical attitude has kept many analysts from showing their spirit and temperament for fear it would be 'suggestion' or 'advice' and therefore unscientific. If we can judge from this root *iatros*, it is the task of the healer to inspire, animate, and kindle emotion. When the analyst does this he may be actually more the physician in the old sense than is his detached medical colleague.

The emotional involvement with the patient is brought out in other European words for the physician: *läkare* (Swedish), *lekarz* (Polish), *lekar* (Serbian, and similar in other Slavic languages). The radical of these terms is the same as found in the Latin *loqui*, to speak, from which we have 'eloquence' and 'loquacious'. Affiliated through the same radical is both the rational discourse of the Greek *lekein* and the affective voice of animal nature *laskein* (to cry), Lithuanian *loti* (howl), Latin *latrare* (the crying of a dog). The task of the medical man was, according to these roots, akin to that of the medicine man. The affective level of treatment through incantation, prayer, and lament aided the primitive physician to drive out the demons. He took part with his voice and *spoke from levels below rational knowledge*. He even let the same demons possess him, taking on the patient's illness as his own.

Of all these linguistic deracinations, the change in meaning which 'pathology' has undergone is the most revealing. Literally, pathology means the *logos* of *pathos*, which is perhaps best translated as the study of suffering. The Indo-Germanic root of pathos is *spa*, to be found in the modern German word *spannen*, *spannung*= long drawn-out, as the tension of a bow-string. From the same root come 'patient' and 'patience'. Both are long-enduring, and, as the alchemists said, "in your patience is your soul". The eradication of pathology in the modern sense of doing away with disease, when applied to the psyche means as well doing away with tension and suffering, with the patience to endure, and eventually, with the soul.

That the physician's patients try his patience is more than a weary pun. In his patience is his soul, and in his patients is the soul of medicine. How the physician meets his patients, understands their pathology, tolerates suffering and tension and restrains his *furor agendi*, reveals his own patience and depth of soul.

The aim of this digression has been to point to another side in words basic to the medical profession. This other, older side is philosophical on the one hand, and emotional on the other. It points to meditation and a kind of emotional participation, both of which transcend the too narrowly intellectual view of the physician as natural scientist. This other side approximates to the attitude of the analyst, who investigates nature by understanding man. Until the physician has found his way back to his earlier and more integrated view of his calling, a medical prerogative on words such as 'therapy', 'doctor', 'patient', etc., ought not to hold, nor should the medical opinion as to who or what is lay in psychotherapy be considered valid.

CHAPTER VIII

THE HEALER AS HERO

LET us enquire why, from the perspective of medicine, suicide is to be prevented, disease opposed, and death postponed. Could there be a root metaphor, an archetypal attitude, which shapes the physician's perspective and guides his activity? We have spoken of this attitude as a dread of death and have found signs of it affecting the physician's work from behind the scenes through his unconscious. It is likely that this dread corresponds with an archetypal vision in the psyche, not of death alone, but of unconsciousness.

A metaphor combining dread of unconsciousness and dread of death can be found in the archetypal symbolism of the Great Mother. Even the masculine representations of death (as can be read in Herzog) have usually a dark and earthy cast that is affiliated with a devouring, omnipotent Goddess. The enemy of death is the hero standing for light and air and sky, a Sun God, the principle of consciousness.

The more materialistically we take the vision of death in the psyche, the more concrete will be the hero's weapon and the more physically visible will be the principle of consciousness. When death is conceived only as material organic death, then the principle of consciousness must be carried by one who meets the challenge physically, on the organic level. Therefore the prime carrier of the death-fighter image today is the physician. The principle of consciousness, of light and air and sky, has been materialised into his gleaming surgical and rainbow-hued pharmaceutical instruments, purged by fire and spirit of all chthonic impurities.

The physician draws his power from this archetype. It is not his knowledge which gives him the hero's mantle, for the physician knows fundamentally little more than others know about life and death, as many an old consultant will readily admit, and as many an enquiring patient and young practitioner have discovered, bitterly. Nor is it his devotion and sacrifice that gives the heroic aura. Others, even coal miners, have codes of loyalty and run as many risks without being ennobled by this image. The physician is numinous because he is the first among fighters against dark death. The fight against the dark is perhaps the first human task; and the battle against the regressive dragon of unconsciousness, the 'jaws of death', is repeated every time the physician splints and bandages or writes a prescription.

Therefore, the physician must treat. Above all else *he must do something*. Were he to do nothing, nothing at all, he would lay down his arms against death and divest himself of his archetypal role. This role has made him effective in the first place. Any passivity on his part becomes a sort of suicide. For him, a therapeutic regression is a contradiction in terms. Healing must be an advance, a thrust against the powers of darkness. He must fight death in others and keep the myth going in himself. It hardly matters what he does as long as he can constellate the image of the saviour, the one who holds death off but a little while longer. Healing means treating.

Experiments with placebos, the varied, sometimes contrary, treatments for certain conditions, and the different schools of medicine (orthodox western, Chinese acupuncture, quackery, home-remedies, witch-doctoring, homeopathy, faith-healing, bone-setting, Christian Science, baths and waters, unorthodox healing, etc.) all show that it is not altogether what the physician does, but *that* he does. This does not mean that the great apparatus of orthodox medicine is useless and that one could as well prescribe leeches and cupping. This is not the point of the argument. Obviously, within the system of operations which Western medicine uses today, certain treatments are preferred. Obviously, scientific medicine is effective. *The point is rather that, contained in the system of operations of any school of healing, there is the archetype of the healer.* It is this healer archetype which gives the physician his numinosity and makes his treatment effective. In other words, healing lies as much in the healer as in the medicine.

The healer archetype has been too narrowly conceived. Particularly narrow is the common view that the healer is the servant of life only. Again, life has been reduced to physiology, whereas the original Greek word *bios* meant the entire life process or course of a life, not just its bodily functioning. Not life but *light is the healer's true God.* The healer represents consciousness; he is the light-bringing hero. The Greek God of healers, Asklepios, is son of Apollo. Asklepios himself is not one of the great pantheon. He is an offspring of the sun-god—only one of the ways the light of consciousness performs in the world. The healer archetype does not depend upon any specific mode or method of medicine, as long as the mode through which it shines furthers consciousness. Clarification, enlightenment, insight and vision, concentration of experience, as well as broader spiritual horizons also serve Apollo. Healing may as well come about through the dialectic of analysis and need not be confined to the concrete techniques of physical medicine.

With the secularisation of medicine, the Gods are no longer real. Dead Gods can hardly heal. Today, only the physician can heal, and that is why he carries so much and is always driven to do something. He is his own agent, and healing comes about through his actions. Once he was an agent of the Gods, passive to their intentions. In

Asklepian medicine, a system of healing lasting for at least one thousand years (and still operative in contemporary analysis, as Meier indicates), the healer was quite passive, when compared with the modern physician's rage for action. The Gods gave the disease and the Gods took it away when the time was ripe. (Frequently, the time was never ripe, or rather, ripeness was death itself and so the cure was death.) Then, it was Apollo who acted. According to Kerenyi, one of his epithets, *bonthei*, meant he 'hastened to help.' The physician was the God's assistant, serving the natural healing process in the light of his knowledge. But this light was never a replacement for the process itself; knowledge was not healing. Today, the physician contends alone with life and death, because the Gods are dead—or so he believes. He has taken over from the Gods, and a mark of his assumption to a divine place is his hastening to help, his rage for action, his *furor agendi*.

Although the physician is still carried by his root metaphor, he has lost relation to it, so that at times Apollo would seem to possess him and drive medicine towards an ever-increasing desire for light, order, reason, moderation, and harmonious, unemotional perfection. The physician worships these principles, and every new hospital is a temple to the secularised Apollo. The high priests make their rounds followed by their white retinue, passing among the sick suppliants, dispensing orders in the jargon of a cult. Less and less does the physician leave this precinct to enter by home visits the irrational, unsterile world of the sufferer. More and more, those two great moments of life, birth and death, take place within the physician's sanctuary, which was of course set up primarily neither for birth nor death, but for disease.

The analyst, when investigating the unconscious, must be wary of undue influence from Apollo. The dark is not

Apollo's first realm. Apollonic consciousness tends to recoil in dread from the unconscious, identifying it with death. Medical analysis with its Apollonic background will use dialectic too intellectually, too much as technique. The analyst finds himself trying to produce order, reason, and detachment in his patient. He tries to clear up problems, by bringing the unconscious to light. He takes pride in explaining mechanisms and aims for balance and harmony. Above all, he tends to work detachedly, from a lofty all-knowing Olympic throne.

If Apollo is detachment and clarity, Dionysos is involvement. In his need for Apollo the analyst might be led to antagonise Apollo's opposite, Dionysos. If the analyst is to keep one foot in and one foot out, as in meeting the suicide risk, he is wise to have one standpoint provided by each God.

The tales of Dionysos show this other standpoint. Where Apollo is moderation, Dionysos is exaggeration, of which orgy is the best example. He appears in the form of bull, lion, panther, and serpent. His femininity is pronounced. He was celebrated in dance and honoured as patron of the drama which had therapeutic intentions. Participants in the Dionysion mysteries dismembered and ate the God and drank him as wine. One incorporated the divine spirit into oneself or entered his spirit through intoxicated orgy, joyous dance, and the passions of a drama.

When an analyst works from within his emotions where he is most dark and attached himself, and works with a spirit that rises from instinct, he is following this opposite of Apollo. This approach is hardly possible for medicine unless it were to take up the methods of the witch-doctor. This altogether different approach to the unconscious is also one-sided. But here, at least the realm of the dark is no longer identified with the Great Mother and experienced with dread as it must be from the perspective of the sun-hero. With the help of Dionysos an analyst is better able to get caught by the drama of the patient, to enter madness and be torn apart, to let the woman in him show, to admit his animal shape and be impelled by the brute drives of power, of raw laughter, of sexual passion, and the thirst for more and more. Dionysos offers involvement in suffering, and the mark of the hero-healer here would be that ability to undergo in oneself *the trials of emotion* and through these emotions find an identification with the same powers in the other.

The opposites—left hand, right hand; one foot in and one foot out—maintain the tension of consciousness in the analyst. Too much one way or the other—detachment or involvement—and the analyst has slid unconsciously into an archetypal role. The Apollonic role is the most dangerous for him, because it tends to reach him unawares through the medical background of the profession. Then he becomes the heroic healer, opposing, preventing, and dreading the confusions which the patient has brought to him to heal.

In fact, the analyst is not the Healer. There are no Healers; there are only those through whom the healer archetype works, through whom Apollo and Dionysos speak. An analyst appears as Healer only to the distorted vision of the ill, because the ill cannot find the source of healing in themselves. They can no longer hear the voices nor understand the language of the healing powers in the unconscious. So an analyst must mediate between them and the Gods—and, perhaps, between the Gods themselves. If an analyst identifies with the divine role of Healer he forces the analysand into an identification with the compensatory role of Patient. Then analysis becomes interminable, the analyst requiring the patient as strongly as the patient needs him. Because health and healing mean etymologically the same as 'whole', health could never depend upon any other person. The patient must remain Patient as long as he looks to the Healer for what he has not found, that is, his own relation to the Gods. Health, like wholeness, is completion in individuality, and to this belongs the dark side of life as well: symptoms, suffering, tragedy, and death. *Wholeness and health therefore do not exclude these 'negative' phenomena*; they are requisite for health. We can begin to see how differently an analyst relates to the healer archetype than does his modern medical colleague too influenced by the Apollonic tradition.

The tradition of detachment is anyway rather new in medicine. Previously medicine was closer to what analysis is today, embracing body and soul, Apollonic and Dionysion. In all cultures and in ours until recently physicians served Gods as priests; now the priesthood remains, and the temples, but where are the Gods? The new religion of the enlightenment has enthroned reason and body at the expense of eros and soul. And it is just in the neglected area of eros and soul, not in rational technique, that modern medicine finds its predicaments: over-specialisation, house-calls, fees, hospital administration, medicine in politics, medical education, the doctor-patient relationship—and all those issues which show how the human aspect has fallen into the shadow.

Much of the problem has to do with the repression of the Dionysion, that essential element in healing as emphasised in all medicine until recent times. One is led to suppose that the contemporary physician has not been spared today's body problem and that he is no more at home with the flesh than are his charges. He alone cannot be blamed for his materialism and his escape to laboratory and surgery, where mind and body can be so cleanly cut apart. We all do the same in different ways in the age of Apollonic science and Dionysion acting-out in affect and fantasy. The physician carries the burden and our disappointment only because he carries the image of the healer, and we so desperately need to be healed. We expect him somehow to show the way by finding his way back to the archetypal image of the healer. Then the analyst would not be forced way out to those extreme positions of 'only soul', 'only eros', 'only emotion'. Then, a true medical analysis could be founded in the spirit of healing in the name of both Gods.

CHAPTER IX

THE PATHOLOGICAL BIAS

PATHOLOGY studies the inception and evolution of morbid states. It has been defined as that branch of science concerned with the search for the cause and mechanism of disease. The usual concept of disease has been established by abstracting those characteristics of the sick which differ from the normal. Pathology tells of disorders of Bios, the process of life. There is both organic pathology and psychopathology.

As we have seen above, pathology means originally the study of suffering; yet in modern pathology the suffering of the subject, his complaint, is only one factor contributing to the data determining disease. It is not at all the central factor, and much of the work of pathology is carried out by people who have never seen the patient, but only bits of his material substance. As each patient presents subjective variables that distort microscopic precision, the medical pathologist finds it best to leave the sufferer out of the picture as much as possible in order to name the disease quickly and exactly. Owing to the influence of pathology, medicine has become more and more an intellectual challenge, less and less an emotional relation between doctor and patient. By shifting focus from the bedside to the laboratory, or by letting the laboratory methods of pathology influence his clinical attitudes, the physician takes over a pathological bias. This bias would lead him to believe that diseases exist apart from human beings and that the study of disease in itself is more appropriate than is the study of the diseased human being.

When an analyst shifts interest away from the complainer to the complaint and its cause, he too has moved from bedside to laboratory. He too has begun to suffer a pathological bias. This shift is more serious in analysis than in medicine, because in medicine there are conditions that can be isolated *in vitro* where also an anti-toxin, say, can be developed and only as an end stage applied to the patient. But in analysis there are no parasites, infecting agents, or chemical components apart from the patient. There is no *in vitro* situation, no other place to look, because *the disease is the patient*.

When the pathologist attempts to solve 'the riddle of life' even the advanced histo-chemist still proceeds by the classic methods of anatomy, which is to separate separable things, or, as Claude Bernard said: "to dissociate all the complex phenomena successively into more and more simple phenomena". This leads to increased differentiation of parts (as in nuclear physics), which in turn requires more refined technical equipment. The organism in its whole life situation is no longer central because it is complex. And this complex cannot be grasped by a specialist. Medicine tends towards developing new instruments and techniques for dissociating that complex, the patient. Simpler phenomena are usually to be found by going backwards towards origins. This is the *genetic approach* to explaining problems. Processes, like disease, are investigated in their simplest infancy, not in terms of the ends they achieve, since the end is always that general state, Death. The embryonic therefore tends to be more interesting than the mature, and childhood is given more weight than old age.

This genetic approach has had an unhappy effect on psychotherapy. Psychological disorder comes to mean childhood disorder, and the search is on for dissociating the present into the past, the complex into the simple, the psychological into material traumata. We race backwards along the rails of this fallacious model towards simpler earlier events, coming to a halt finally at that only other surety besides death—Mother. So many of the phenomena of analysis are now interpreted in terms of the mother–child relation that one must ask whether psychotherapy is not suffering from a collective unconscious mother-complex. This 'diagnosis' fits in with its causal genetic approach imitative of natural science, and what is matter in science is mother in psychology.

When the anatomical or genetic approaches do not get to the root causes as had been hoped, then the pathological bias must attack its problems through *measurement*. The simplest way to differentiate things is to measure, for every material event exists in some quantity and therefore can be measured. Health and disease can be expressed in formulae: blood-count, basal metabolism, etc. Unhappily, as we have already seen, this approach tends to reduce qualitative differences to differences of quantity. This brings with it another philosophy: the good life tends to mean more life. Promoting life begins to mean prolonging it. The development of consciousness begins to mean greater performance. Methods of pathology carried in the blood-stream of medicine thus begin to infect psychotherapy.

In medicine the more quickly and surely the pathology is recognised, the better the chances for quick and sure treatment. For this reason, the physician is always on the lookout for pathology. If he is to be an efficient diagnostician, on which depends the course of his work, the possibility of unsuspected disorder must affect everything he hears from the patient and everything he observes. Anything may be symptomatic; suspicion belongs. If an analyst carries on with this medical attitude it is a pathological bias.

When is a person ill? When is a person mentally ill? Medical books state often enough that the borderlines of even organic pathology are not clear. There are levels of complexity; that is, there are diseases like rabies and small-pox where individual variables are less important than is the pathological syndrome which is fairly accounted for by its proximate causes. But more complex conditions, like suicide, require fuller models of causality to be comprehended. There is a difference between straightforward pathological conditions that can be explained through one part of the human system and other conditions which can never be explained, but only understood in terms of the whole system and its environment. Applying a simpler model to complex conditions twists nature to a pre-fabricated frame. It is a pathological bias.

To find the borderlines between health and disease, one must look more carefully at the medical idea of health. It is generally conceived as proper functioning, physical well-being, soundness of structure, absence of morbidity, freedom from disorder or disability, etc. Clearly, as Dubos has said, this idea of health is utopian; it allows no place for the realities of human health, which include disorder and suffering at every turn. 'Health' so conceived only provides ground for the pathological bias and the regressive prescriptions of modern psychiatry, the anodynes, tranquillisers, and entertainments. Suffering so belongs to the human lot that one can say it is more 'normal' than is ideal health, or, let us say, *suffering is normal health*. If so, then where does pathology begin? One-third to two-thirds of the complaints the physician meets in practice show no strict pathology at all. In complex conditions the definition of illness is as vague as is the definition of health. This vagueness is even more pronounced when the subjective side, the complaint, is given more value. There can be objective pathological evidence and no complaints, complaint and no pathological evidence. Inside and outside may present quite different signs.

For the physician a prime sign of pathology is pain. The old-fashioned rational physician identified pain and suffering. Where there was no demonstrable organic base to suffering it was simply imaginary. Pain had to be the basis of suffering, as if Christ's cry came from his physical wounds. Today, we know that suffering precedes pain; it is the psyche that translates physiological events into painful sensations. Alter consciousness, as in hypnosis, and fakirs walk on coal or dentists drill holes, painlessly. Suffering can be present without basis in organic pain, and even pain can be present without organic basis (phantom pain). But there can be no pain unless it be suffered by the psyche. This means *suffering is primary to pain*, pain being but a fuse—albeit the major one—to set off suffering.

Besides the physical approach aimed at removing the cause of pain, pain can be attacked psychologically in only two ways. We may increase the capacity to endure suffering in the Spartan or Stoic mode. Psychological techniques tend in this direction. Or we may decrease our sensitivity with anodynes in the modern fashion. This leads to a constriction of the capacity to endure, which in turn reduces our tolerance for all sorts of suffering. The vicious circle which then commences leads not to decreased sensitivity, but instead to a heightened susceptibility to suffering so that anodynes become even more imperative. With this begins a chronic hypochondriasis and the drug-and-distraction dependency of our age. *The pathological bias has confused pain with suffering, numbing us to both.* The message which suffering would announce is annulled and the purposes of our psychic pains are prevented from entering awareness.

This has led some analysts to take up the counter position: abjuring all physical treatments. But then they too are caught by the pathological bias. They too are confusing suffering with pain. In their recognition of the value of suffering, they mistakenly believe that pain must be reduced *in extremis* only. In their affirmation of suffering for fuller consciousness, they forget that consciousness can be radically limited by pain.

Suffering is necessary for increased awareness and the development of personality. We were led to this conclusion in the discussion of the death experience. How many opportunities for awareness the idealistic definition of health has hindered we can never know. We can assume that many a death experience, because of the concomitant anguish, was stopped short by the pathological bias which allows no place for suffering in its picture of health. What this same idea of health has done to the physician's own development is also an unhappy thought.

If mal-functioning and suffering are viewed only pathologically, the physician prevents himself from sensing his own wound. In antiquity the physician healed through his own suffering, as Christ healed through his. The wound that would not heal was the well of cures. The purpose of training analysis is not merely to heal the personality of the analyst, but to open his wounds from which his compassion will flow. But the physician no longer works emotionally, because his predilection for scientific pathology tends to remove him from the understanding of suffering in favour of the explanation of disease. He no longer applies the ancient maxim: physician, cure thyself. Physicians are notoriously bad patients, perhaps because they have lost the ability to be wounded. The idea of health has been so falsified that the physician cannot cure himself by beginning with his own psychic infections, wounds, and dreads. The logos of suffering cannot be described by a pathology textbook which uses clinical terms for soul experiences; it belongs also to the fields of religion, philosophy, and psychology.

As pain and suffering differ, so harming and wounding are not the same. When the analyst keeps alive his own wounds he is not harming himself. When the soul history returns again and again to basic painful wounds, the fundamental complexes, it is to draw new meanings from them. Each return reopens them and starts their weeping afresh, yet this in no way conflicts with the maxim *primum nihil nocere*. Should an analyst think so and try to suture the wounds in himself or patient and say that this or that is a closed chapter, he is again acting medically. The wrong cure, or the right cure at the wrong time, does more harm than the open wound. The wound, as poetry often tells us, is a mouth and the therapist need only listen.

A usual way of determining pathology is through collective standards. Certain conditions are pathological only collectively. With smallpox, for example, there is no difference between individual and collective; with suicide there is. Epidemic suicide as preached by Hegesias in Roman Egypt had to be met with collective action. But epidemic psychic phenomena are not individual acts. Applying collective standards or collective measures to behaviour that is primarily individual shows a pathological bias.

The physician is obliged to use collective standards. For one thing, epidemiology is his field. He stands not just for his patient's life; he stands as well for the life of society, for public health. This task cannot ever be overestimated. Prevention is basic to public health, and a pathological bias helps medicine search for pathology in sanitation, in food and drugs, in air and water. Furthermore, collective methods of establishing disease are very relevant for medical diagnosis.

Since a subjective complaint may be unverifiable by

objective examination, and since objective pathological evidence may be so tenuous, or even altogether lacking, medicine has another method besides subjective complaint and objective evidence. This is statistical pathology. The concept of disease is based on abstracting those characteristics of the morbid which differ from the normal. Pathology says frankly that abnormal changes are merely deviations from the norm.

Deviations from the normal depend upon a defined norm. Deviations depend upon where one puts the limits of normality, how wide the middle part of a curve is drawn. Half the daily decisions the practitioner makes are about complaints without organic basis, complaints for which there are no objectively given norms. The deviations from the norm in these cases therefore tend to be deviations from the practitioner's norm. The physician gets his norm from his medical training, his clinical experience, his current reading; and for complex psychological conditions, his norm tends to be based upon his personal tolerance, the extent of his dread. Unlike the analyst, he has not exposed these norms to assessment. They remain as a pathological bias between him and the norms of the patient, which may be altogether different.

The word 'normal' comes from the Greek *norma*, which was a carpenter's square, that right-angled tool for establishing straightness. From such a tool there will, of course, be 'deviations', and everything not 'straight' and 'square' will be pathological. Normal merges indistinguishably with healthy. The widespread use of the word 'deviation' in politics, in sex, in technology attests to the influence of the statistical norm upon the pathological bias. Our conception of normal tends to be based on statistical expectations. What exceeds or falls short deviates from the norm. The more intellectually severe the physician's mind, the less able it is to cope with psychological variables. Medical statistics limit tolerance and increase dread towards those conditions at the extreme ends of the curve, that is, the more individual phenomena. Medical training is lacking in the knowledge gained from the study of the humanities—history, literature, biography—which show the meaning of situations that deviate from the norm. Expectations that are only statistical are no longer human. As Jung has pointed out in his last major work, *The Undiscovered Self*, no single human being fits the statistical norm. We are each sick because a pathological bias is built into the statistical model.

The pathological bias works in yet another way. This is what the French call *déformation professionnelle*. Seeing life through one's profession is one of the results of professional training. The scribe is orderly, the bureaucrat indecisive, the tailor sees the stitching not the man. One becomes identified with the role one plays, the persona one wears; outside moves inside and determines outlook.

For medicine this twist of vision means seeing pathology first. 'First' means seeing the pathological both *before* anything else and *behind* everything else, the hidden before the evident. For example, in Freudian analysis sexual pathology lies behind much of man and culture. Psychotherapy has been distorted by this bias, and daily life itself has been bent awry. Friendship is latent homosexuality; and behind every monument of culture stand incest-longings, sadism, anality, penis-envy, castration anxiety, and the like. In Existentialism, nausea, dread, boredom, and loneliness are at the core of actions. In Marxism the achievement of history can be traced back to slavery, persecution, exploitation, and war. The pathological reduces the best to the worst.

This is a muddle of models. Spatial location is confused with a scale of values. The first is the simplest, the simplest is the lowest, the lowest is the worst. The ultimate of everything always points backwards to beginnings, to the first link in a causal chain. Ultimately we are only animals, or cells, or biochemical blends. Expressed psychologically, we are told that we are ultimately only what happened during the first years of life. Psychology in depth tends to mean psychology at its lowest, simplest, most remote from here and now. Dreams are examined for their latent, not manifest, content. Then, when the worst and lowest has been uncovered, it is presumed that the ultimate (simplest and most basic) has also been found.

However, we are also ultimately what we become, what we are at death. In one sense death is more real than birth in that all beginnings are behind us. Death is immediately present because the moment of death can be every moment and is every moment to the transforming soul, which lives through perishing. There is no moral problem about the past except repentance. There is no 'how' to enter life, but there is a 'how' to enter death. The pathological bias reduces events anatomically downwards to their simplest elements and views phenomena from their back-sides.

For example, suicide occurs largely within the usual human setting, yet it is conceived in its pathological caricature, as among interned psychotics. It is approached where it is least understandable, where it is complicated by organic and other endogenic factors about which psychiatry has anyway few answers. And the old psychiatric fallacy is perpetuated: the soul is approached through its abnormality. What is discovered is then applied everywhere. As Chavigny, the French psychiatrist, put it: *"Tout suicide doit être interpreté au point de vue psychiatrique."* And Eissler completes this: "... to prevent a patient's suicide is the self-evident duty of a psychiatrist and needs no further justification or discussion" (p. 165). All suicides are ultimately the same sick one. Each suicide, like all suffering, contains opposite seeds; there is, of course, shadow to every act and pathology everywhere. But the bias seizes the sick one first, finding the root of every act to lie in shadow.

An analyst who works from this muddled medical model of depth psychology will probably find his patients for ever feeling guilty. No matter how they try, they seem never able to get to the bottom of their problems, and should they once arrive at this bottom it would be a nether-world of bestiality. The patient cannot be plucked loose from this evil ground as long as the analyst reduces events to ultimates and finds these ultimates at the lowest level only. The analyst's own pathological bias becomes transplanted to the patient, producing metastases in every corner of the patient's personality. The shadow is everywhere and the patient worries over his responsibility for all the evil he carries with him, whereas much of this darkness is cast by the shadow of the analyst from the bias of his stance.

Perhaps a psychological bias might do medicine less harm than the pathological bias does analysis. Every event, including the organic diseases within medicine's own province, would have a dark side. And this other side would be its unconscious, psychological aspect.

A theory of disease called "attenuated infection" has been recently argued in detail by H. J. Simon. According to this theory, man and microbe live together in peaceful co-existence to their mutual benefit. Host and parasite are part of the same larger system, so that infection is continuous (attenuated) and habitual. When the infecting agent is from another ecological field, as in rabies and plague, there is no natural coexistence. But pathogenic viruses, intestinal bacteria, tuberculosis, staphylococcus and streptococcus infections form part of our living system.

Specific measures against them—radiation, surgery, antibiotics—disrupt the attenuated infection, disturb the co-existence, and at times are the causes of new symptoms and infections. These new diseases have even been called "iatrogenic", that is, diseases caused by the physician. Because the physician continues to link infection with disease and disease with death, he fights—and in the end often defeats his own purpose.

The theory of attenuated infection says that an infectious agent is necessary for disease in the host, but it is not sufficient for disease to break out. The germs may be present but the disease not. Even where the agent is identified, the occasion for falling ill is a riddle. Euphemisms such as 'lowered resistance' and 'homeostatic imbalance' tell us little. *To get the sufficient conditions for disease we must turn to an investigation of the host.* Here, a psychological bias might help. It asks: What meaning has this disease at this moment in the patient's life? What is going on in the unconscious of the patient and in his environment? What seems to be the purpose of the disease; what is it interrupting or serving? *The bias of psychology assumes that the disease is achieving something.* It would propose entirely new sorts of research programmes. In short, the pathological bias may see illness where there is none and be unable to account for illness when it is actually present, while a psychological bias might give information which pathology itself cannot provide.

A first step in correcting the astigmatism of orthodox medicine and bringing a new focus would be a psychological bias on the part of every physician. This might break the vicious circle both of iatrogenic disease and of recurrent illness. Even more, it might lead the physician to take up psychology, beginning with the analysis of his own personality, of his own wounds, with the same dedication that becomes his calling.

The theory of attenuated infection, the ideas of Jaspers and von Weizacker on the biographical significance of disease, the approach of Clark-Kennedy, of Dubos, as well as other holistic concepts, present the practice of medicine in another, more psychological light. This light is less brilliantly focused, but it illumines a wider area. It sees not just the affected part retracted under the surgeon's lamps, but the human being in the situational crisis of his disease. The physician can no longer get rid of pathology without, paradoxically, a psychological bias *that does not aim to get rid of it at all.* By preferring to consider analysis as lay medicine, medicine avoids coming to terms with the one field which offers it the most towards solving its two most urgent problems: the significance of disease and the doctor–patient relationship. To put it another way, the medical practitioner could profit from becoming lay himself. If lay means unprofessional, then lay means open. The prejudices of the professional attitude and the rigid model of medical thinking could be set aside in order to turn to the riddles of the patient with an open ear. Until medicine meets the challenge of analysis and lets its thinking be penetrated and fertilised by the reality of the unconscious, its ideas are not of this century, and its progress will continue to be only technical—chemical, surgical, instrumental—while its mind remains cloistered in virginity, walking through the white hospital halls with quaint notions of suffering, of causality, of disease and death.

CHAPTER X

DIAGNOSIS AND THE ANALYTICAL DIALECTIC

Does diagnosis truly belong among the main tasks of the physician as reviewed in Chapter II? Does diagnosis not rather serve more fundamental aims, such as preventing, treating, repairing—or the general one of promoting life? For thousands of years diagnosis has been, and still is in many places today, rudimentary or simply wrong. Different systems of medicine recognise clinical signs differently. Nevertheless, physicians were and are able to treat and heal, to repair and encourage, to promote life. The history of medicine shows diagnosis to have been grossly inadequate in the past. Yet how effective have been medical practitioners! This discrepancy between medical theory and practice can be partly accounted for by the healer archetype, as we have seen above.

Diagnosis takes a secondary place in the healing art because medicine is an *applied* science; it stands or falls with its effects upon the patient. There can be no pure science of diagnosis, of medical knowledge, because there is no medicine without disease and no disease without a patient. As an applied science, the art and method of the physician is first. The physician's knowledge may be less important than his actions, especially his ability to constellate healing. Again, it may be less important what the physician does than *that* he does.

But diagnosis has moved more and more to the centre of modern medicine. This is in part owing to the influence of the natural sciences upon medicine, especially since the seventeenth century. The significance of diagnosis reflects the ever-growing role of knowledge in medicine, over and against its art and practice. Scientific medicine searches for the causes of clinical signs, which when found determine the course of treatment. Correct diagnosis requires knowledge, and this knowledge grows more complex, as eleven million pages of medical journal text are added to the literature yearly. The physician is obliged to turn away from the patient and to the laboratory for his diagnosis, because in the laboratory this complex and immense knowledge can be systematised and condensed. Clinical signs tend to become laboratory reports, that is, through the examination of X-ray pictures, EEG and ECG charts, blood and urine analysis, etc., the practitioner puts together his diagnosis. So too for his treatment, the physician turns to the laboratory, which has prepared products to meet the diagnostic categories.

The physician thus has become an intermediary between patient and researcher, and by withdrawing his personality as much as possible, he keeps from obstructing the passage of accurate information from patient to laboratory and correct prescription back from laboratory to patient. Diagnostic computer machines for improving the accuracy of diagnosis and prescription are the logical outcome of the scientific evolution of medicine. As long as the physician tries to approximate the viewpoint of the physicist by assuming the model of thought of the natural sciences, he must keep 'out' as much as possible by defining sharply the 'cut' between himself and patient. He must remain an objective observer of the processes going on in the patient and shield these events from subjective interference. The best physician therefore is the one who is least in the situation. Transferred to psychotherapy, the best analyst would be the one who, in the orthodox model, sits behind the patient, rarely speaks, and keeps his own personality under cover.

Does not academic and clinical psychology show the same pattern? Thousands of diagnostic tests have been invented in the last decades in order to provide accurate, laboratory-like information to the practitioner. This knowledge is meant to aid diagnostic classification and facilitate choice of treatment. The test situation is like the laboratory situation; participation of the psychologist must be reduced to a minimum. For accurate knowledge one must eliminate factors arising from personal sympathies. It would seem that knowledge and understanding are incompatible. As understanding, with its sympathetic intuitive involvement with another, has fallen away because it could not be trusted from the scientific point of view, the evaluation of another person has come more and more to depend upon diagnostic tools. Can this sort of knowledge ever compensate for the loss of understanding?

The conflicts which arise in clinical teams between psychiatrist and social worker reflect this difference between knowledge and understanding. When the interviewer or test psychologist knows his subject well and has established rapport, his observation may no longer be objective enough. It has no longer the same diagnostic validity.

The dialectic of analysis, on the other hand, attempts to overcome the distance between subject and observer by weaving bonds which pull the two nearer. This begins only when it is no longer quite clear who is subject and who is observer. The patient begins to observe himself and the analyst, thus taking part in the dialectic; and the analyst, by being subjected to the on-going process, is no longer an observer making a diagnosis.

Both diagnosis and dialectic start from the known and work with the unknown. Both use the intellect and both require response from the patient. However, where diagnosis comes to a stop when the unknown has been made known, when the disease has been classified, dialectic continues on into the unknown and does not come to a stop. It corresponds with the endless process of becoming conscious, beyond the restrictions of rational intellect.

This difference between diagnosis and dialectic shows again in the difference between *cure* and *consciousness*. The end of clinical treatment is cure. The process comes to a fruit and all medical measures are stages towards this fulfilment. Consciousness, however, as far as we can read the evidence, comes to no definite goal, no final fruition, but is a continuous on-going process. An analyst who has a notion of cure as the goal of his work is thinking medically. He has not grasped the nature of the complex, the basis of the analytical process. There are no antidotes for complexes. They cannot be cured away because *complexes are not causes*, though they be the determinants of psychic life. They are basic, given with the soul itself, as energetic nuclei and qualitative foci of psychic life. A medical model tends to conceive them like wounds and traumata, or as malignant growths and foreign bodies to be removed in the medical manner. But if complexes are energetic centres, they cannot be 'cured' without damaging the vitality of the patient. When an analyst proceeds with this end in mind he finds cure tends to show itself in his patients becoming more coolly ordered, less vibrant and free. (People in the arts have always feared that medical analysis might remove their complexes and by cauterising their wounds castrate their creativity.) As energetic centres, complexes rather than cured or killed may be transformed, and as purposeful entelechies the dialectic with them develops their dynamism and furthers consciousness.

Does this mean that each analysis must be 'eternal' because the dialectic for consciousness seems to have no end?

143

Rather, it means that the dialectic of the *analytical process* goes on at least as long as life. This process, strange to say, is only secondarily a result of the actual analysis between the two partners. The dialectic goes on within the soul of each person, between the ego and the unconscious dominants, those major psychic forces which shape character and guide fate. *The dialectic is there before the analysis begins*, and shows itself often as symptoms, whenever it has not been taken up and replied to positively by the ego. The soul's development proceeds through tensions, where at one moment the weight is with the ego and at the next is with the unconscious. Psychic energy is like an alternating current that is intensified by analysis. The analyst provides the opposite pole when the patient has lost contact with the opposite in himself. Then, all the split-off forces of the patient's unconscious become constellated in analysis. Like a magnet, the analyst seems to draw them to him. He stands for the unconscious of the patient, now out there in the open, so that the analyst becomes a chief occupation of the patient, and we have what is called 'transference'. This goes on until, through dialectic, the analysand can objectify the realities of the soul *without needing the person of the analyst to do this for him*. He then can maintain the process of intensifying consciousness alone, occasionally returning to an analyst to work on a particularly unorganised field of energy.

The dialectician acts like a midwife, said Socrates, who invented the method. His presence aids the patient to be delivered of the new life evolving out of himself. *The analyst furthers a process which is fundamentally the analysand's own*. Primary to all interpersonal relations is the intrapersonal dialectic, the relation to the unconscious psyche.

The dialectic proceeds as well within each of the partners separately. The analyst, too, has dreams, emotions, symptoms, which he must keep in touch with, as the physician 'keeps up' with the recent literature. An analyst thus tries to practise the maxim of 'physician, cure thyself', applying his own medicine upon himself. He tries to maintain his own consciousness in order not to be unconscious with each of his patients. If he begins to slip, he falls into the roles they put him in. Then they can no longer distinguish between their projections and the analyst's reality, because the analyst has become identified with their own fantasies. Only by maintaining his own pole through his own dialectic with his own dreams, fantasies, emotions, and symptoms can he be of service to the analysand.

Analysis approaches the body as source of symptoms and emotions differently from medicine. The diagnostic approach treats the body as an object. Diagnosis requires meticulous study of this object. Here, the non-medical analyst is absolutely lay. He cannot knowledgeably thump a chest or palpate a belly. This medical ignorance was the major reason why the non-medical analyst—even though he compensate with the necessary learning of organic psychiatry—was considered lay. He could not diagnose; he did not know the body.

Besides being an object, the body is also an experience. The body is both 'it' and 'me'. The body experience goes beyond the notion of a 'body-image'. The experience of the body is in the background of all awareness and the inner sense of one's outer reality. When the patient presents his body for diagnosis he succeeds in withdrawing himself out of it, joining with the examining physician in a detached study of himself on the table. Or he cowers naked, feeling himself haplessly sacrificial, inwardly exposed. These basic reactions show the split which the diagnostic approach constellates. Body becomes only object or only subject. Whereas actually, the body is a sub-jective object and an objective subject. These experiences of the body—especially separation from it and observa-tion of it—are what analysis works to transform. The analyst therefore is cautious about using a diagnostic ap-proach, which, for all its value in medicine, only splits wider what analysis aims to heal.

Analysis too pays meticulous attention to the body. It observes and listens to *the body as an experience*. The body is the vessel in which the transformation process takes place. The analyst knows that there are no lasting changes unless the body is affected. Emotion always tears at the body, and the light of consciousness requires the heat of emotion. These affections of the body during an analysis are symptomatic—not in the diagnostic sense—of stages in the dialectic. To take them diagnostically and treat them medically might harm the process. The outbreak of skin rashes, circulation disorders, internal organ com-plaints, aches and pains, all reflect new areas of body ex-perience, which must often first come about in the guise of ailments until the body can be heard without having to scream for recognition. The analyst also pays the same careful attention to his own body, listening to cues in his own flesh to aid his dialectic. He tries to sense during the hour when he is tired and hungry, sexually excited, slumped in passivity, irritatedly fidgeting, or developing symptoms and illness. His body is a sounding board. This sensitivity is appropriate to the body as experience and fits the analytical work. Although it is not diagnostic, it is hardly lay.

This leads to a consideration of symptoms from the diagnostic and dialectic points of view. For one the symp-tom is a *clinical sign*, for the other it has *symbolic meaning*. Stomach-aches and head-aches are clinical signs, but they also express different meanings according to the general symbolism of stomach and head in a particular person. In this way the dialectical process gains information from symptoms, just as diagnosis turns to them as signs of pathology. Persistent symptoms such as stuttering, recurrent ulcer, 'smoker's cough' are taken up by the dialectical process, and the integration of this suffering also takes place through the symbol.

Where medicine seeks to cure the symptom because it signifies only mal-functioning, analysis explores the symptom for its symbolic significance. Symptoms are not only functional defects. Like all wounds, they are also impairments which have an archetypal background, that is, humans have suffered in these particular ways as far as history records. Biography, mythology, literature, and lore—not only medicine—provide a background for symptomatology. The sufferer can find sense in his wound by relating to it symbolically. He may even no longer need the reversible symptom once the symbolic aspects of it have entered consciousness. Then, his attention will not be dragged perforce and with pain to the same old gnawing problem. If cure comes about, it is then as a by-product of consciousness.

Diagnosis and dialectic also use different methods. When studying diagnostic signs the physician aims for precision by defining just what is affected, where it hurts, the count and composition of blood, etc. An analyst, on the other hand, attempts to extend the range of consciousness by exploring the symbolic background to symptoms. The method of one is *definition*; of the other, *amplification*.

Definition states what something is and where it is separated from what it is not. Definition excludes by cutting out what does not belong. The more exactly and narrowly something can be defined, the better we know it. As much of the soul is ambiguous and as knowledge about it is still incomplete, sharp definitions are premature. The major problems which the analysand brings to analysis are the major problems of every life: love, family, work, money, emotion, death; and the defining knife may rather maim these problems than free them from their surrounds. Definitions are anyway more appropriate to logic and natural science, where strict conventions about words must be followed and where definitions serve closed systems of operations. The psyche is not a closed system in the same way. Definition settles unease by nailing things down. Analysis is better served by amplification, because it pries things loose from their habitual rigid frames. Amplification confronts the mind with paradoxes and tensions; it reveals complexities. It tends even to build symbols. This gets us closer to psychological truth, which always has a paradoxical unconscious aspect, than does definition with its exclusively conscious rationality.

The method of amplification is rather like the methods of the humanities and the arts. By revolving around the matter under surveillance one amplifies a problem exhaustively. This activity is like a prolonged meditation, or variations on a theme of music, or the patterns of dance or brush-strokes. It has a ritualistic aspect as well, because the dignity of the problem which is being amplified is never wholly claimed by knowledge. One starts off knowing that one cannot know it; one can only hover over it, thrust at it, and pay respects through devoted attention. This permits the levels of meaning in any problem to reveal themselves, and it corresponds to the way the soul itself presents its demands by its iterative returning to basic complexes to elaborate a new variation and urge consciousness on.

The gift of meaning is not the result of interpretation, which so often is but a translation into reasonable words that depotentiate the unconscious. Meaning is not something given by the analyst to a crazy-quilt of dreams and events. It is not put in, but rather brought out. It therefore precedes interpretation and makes interpretation possible, for if meaning were not already there as a potentiality in every psychic event no interpretation would click. Meaning is *a priori*, so that any happening can become a meaningful experience. The analyst brings meaning out in two ways: by laying bare and cutting through to essentials, and by swelling events into pregnancy through amplification.

For the first, he asks questions just like the diagnostician. But in diagnosis questioning aims for precise, factual answers. Just where does it hurt? When did it begin? What is your temperature on waking up? The questions stop when the information has been gained. The questions of analysis do not produce definite answers. Rather they elicit a process that only raises more questions and searches further into life. Meaning is brought out of the unknown. Things are discovered that could hardly be imagined, just as Socrates, through questions, elicited unknown truths out of Meno. The Socratic style of questioning stimulates the soul's questing. Because these questions are life-questions, *such questioning places life itself in question*. Again, we find that the dialectic of the analytical process leads into death experiences.

For the second, amplification leads to new symbols. As old ones become more and more conscious and formulated, the meanings they carry seem to dry. By returning again to the issue through a new turn of amplification—whether it be through reading, through life, through dream—another symbolic aspect is discovered, setting loose another experience. Events take on a symbolic aspect; the inside of life (the *suksma* aspect in Sanskrit) begins to show itself everywhere, an aim of many spiritual disciplines. This leads to deepening the capacity to experience. By growing familiar with the basic complexes of one's soul, one comes to certain truths about oneself. This intimate knowledge is both objective truth and understanding.

Because the themes to which one returns through amplification are not only your and my deepest wounds but are as well the eternal themes of the soul, they can never be settled by definition once and for all. As objective, collective experiences in which each of us participates, we begin also to understand others through reaching the objective, collective levels in our own problems. Training analysis develops objectivity by amplifying the candidate's problems beyond the personal level. He then can comprehend the other person 'from below', as it were.

If understanding were merely sympathy it would be personal. Then indeed only knowledge could lead to truth. This point is most important. Were understanding to be merely an identification with the other's viewpoint and sharing his personal suffering, all judgments about a case would be subjective. The analyst would be trapped in a solipsistic circle of empathy and there would be no objectivity at all. *Analysis would hardly differ from any personal commiseration.* What makes analysis objective and offers the opportunity for a science of the soul is just the soul's objective, collective aspect. This aspect the soul has in common with others, and is shown in the capacity to conceive, image, behave, and be moved according to fundamental metaphors which Jung has called archetypal patterns.

Understanding therefore requires knowledge, *knowledge of the objective psyche.* Without this knowledge of the collective unconscious, the analyst tends to reduce fundamental problems to the personal trivia of an individual life. The dialectic becomes the superficial dialogue of report and memory-chasing, and an exchange of personal opinions. Individuality does not mean this sort of personal differences in detail. The individuality of the soul does not rest upon accidents of upbringing and circumstance, but more probably upon that ability in each of us to discover his particular call of which these accidents form their part and are to be related. This movement towards being what one is meant to be is recognised through a succession of overwhelmingly meaningful experiences which comprise the soul history. (Jung has marked the overall patterns and general stages of these experiences in his researches into the *individuation process* and given personal example of a soul history in his autobiography, *Memories, Dreams, Reflections*.) The analyst tries to understand the other and bring about the other's self-understanding, by relating the case history to the soul history, by placing the trivia in relation to the central myth of the patient's life.

Although the analyst is a specialist, his field, the soul, encompasses nothing less than all of human nature and perhaps even more. The troubles the analyst meets are not merely private and subjective case histories. It is unnecessary modesty for an analyst to describe them as such, and it is insufficient to the full dimension of the troubled soul to use the narrow focus of psychopathological mechanisms and the language of the clinic. The challenges which the soul brings him in practice require him to study. He must know how to place the subjective within an objective psychological context, else he is caught in trivia. And when he speaks out about his work, to use professional language also does the soul injustice. *He has an obligation beyond his speciality, for what walks into his practice is today.* The collective level of the troubled soul is human history. It concerns everybody.

The knowledge of an analyst is taken from philosophy, ethnology, the arts, religion, and mythology in preference to orthodox medicine, because these fields present the formulations of the objective psyche. They report how the soul views and experiences life and death. The problems the analyst is asked to cope with are not curing disease and normalising health, but are the problems of 'how to live' and 'how to die'. A prolonged rich dialectic on these themes will be amplified from many sides. The humanities are more concerned here than are the sciences, and medicine is of less use than myth, where examples with precise detail in imagery and behaviour show how the psyche, at its most fundamental and objective levels, sets up its problems and alternative solutions.

Each dream recapitulates these eternal problems in an eternal language, mixed with the accidental trivia of circumstance. An analyst is obliged to forego reducing either level to the other, but through the dialectic with the dreamer they unite the two. His position of one foot in and one foot out means not only knowledge and understanding, detachment and involvement, but above all an *understanding of the personal level of the psyche in the light of knowledge of the impersonal level*. This provides that *detachment from within*, a sort of symbolic thinking, which is altogether different from having one foot out supported upon a medical pedestal.

CHAPTER XI

HOPING, GROWING, AND THE ANALYTICAL PROCESS

"WHERE there is life, there is hope" is the physician's maxim. Hope puts heart in the patient, strengthening his will to live. The physician dare never yield his hope. It is the essence of his therapeutic attitude.

This maxim means more than its secular, medical use, i.e., as long as the patient lives there is hope for cure. The sentence states an identity of life and hope. Where life is, there is hope. And this hope is the very will to live, the desire for the future—or as the dictionary defines it: "to expect with desire". How could we go on without it; what is tomorrow without it? The physician's maxim offers the idea that man's fundamental driving force might well be hope, just as hopelessness is the atmosphere of suicide. Where there is life, there must be hope. Hope keeps us going. Or as T. S. Eliot has phrased it:

Go, go, go, said the bird: human kind
Cannot bear very much reality.

And if hope is the fundamental emotional force of life, perhaps it is also, as Eliot hints, the opposite: the fundamental deceit, as the expectation and desire that takes us away from the moment.

The tales of the origin of hope in the world might be worth recalling. In India hope belongs to Maya, the Great Goddess, who tempts us with the round of illusion. Like Maya, hope spins the countless fancies of our fate. We are caught up in a web of hopes which is the will to live experienced as projections towards the future. As fundamental emotion, the hope of Maya would be what modern psychology calls the projecting function of the psyche which never lets us go as long as we live, luring us onward. In the West, Pandora is the counterpart of Maya. The tales of their creation show parallels. In Greece, Zeus made Pandora as a life-sized statue, a doll of painted beauty, the first 'sweet cheat' (*kalon kakon*), endowed with virtues by twenty of the Greek divinities. In India, the Great Goddess came into being as a combined product of the assembled Hindu pantheon to save the world from despair. In another tale she appeared in the form of Dawn; and then, as Sati, she was fashioned by Brahma in the presence of twenty divinities to tempt Shiva down from ascetic isolation so that the eternal play of life could continue, breeding and exfoliating without cessation. Associated with the Goddess, Greek and Hindu, are all the follies and vices of human passion, and all the creative (Shiva and Brahma; Prometheus, Hephaestus, Zeus) energies of human pursuits.

Pandora in her original form was represented as a large jar or vessel. As the Panofskys show, this vessel became a box in later tradition. In Pandora, as vessel, all the evils of the world lay concealed. When this was opened (and it must be inevitably, in the same manner that Eve brought Sin into the world by yielding to temptation of the forbidden) out flew the evils, all save Hope. The creation of the phenomenal world of illusion is similar in Greece, in India, in the Old Testament.

Hesiod's tale of Pandora tells us that *hope is one of the evils that was in the vessel, and is the only one that remains within*. It lies concealed where it is not seen, whereas all the other evils, fancies, passions are the projections we meet outside in the world. These can be recaptured by integrating the projections. But hope is within, bound up with the dynamism of life itself. Where hope is, is life.

We can never confront it directly any more than we can seize life, for hope is the urge to live into tomorrow, the heedless leaning ahead into the future. Go, go, go.

Is not religious hope altogether different? We find it in Paul's *Epistle to the Romans*, VIII: "For we are saved by hope: but hope that is seen is not hope: for what a man seeth, why doth he yet hope for? But if we hope for that we see not, then do we with patience wait for it." Hoping is not hoping for what one hopes for; one hopes not for that which is already known. Such hope is hope for the wrong thing. It is illusion. Again to use the words of Eliot:

> *I said to my soul, be still, and wait without hope*
> *For hope would be hope for the wrong thing; wait without love*
> *For love would be love of the wrong thing; there is yet faith*
> *But the faith and the love and the hope are all in the waiting.*

The religious meaning of hope implies the sacrifice of all hoping. Is not this religious hope, in which the waiting is all, the hope of despair that appears when meeting the suicide risk?

Secularised hope shows itself best in medicine. During recent meetings of the American Cancer Society an expert consultant is reported to have explained why the battle to save a patient from cancer must never be given up. No matter the expense, the pain, and the psychic agony, there is always the hope that, during a temporary reprieve, medical science will come up with a remedy and save the patient's life. The quality of life and the entrance into death tend to be placed second to the main medical aim— prolonging life. Life is no longer for the sake of anything else, but has become its own measurement.

This is enough and correct for scientific medicine; but

is it enough and correct for analysis? Saving life has different meanings. For the physician, saving life means first of all postponing death. This is simple and clear. It can be evalued by measurement: by years, days, hours. The hope for salvation which the physician offers is the *hope for more time*, that is, a quantity of life. And the hope the physician serves is the patient's *demand for more life*, not better life, not transformed life. When life becomes its own measurement the good life means simply more life, and death becomes the great evil. And suppose the remedy has been found, flown to the bedside, what hope has the patient? What has been done to save the patient, for his salvation? This sort of medical hope serves secularised salvation—and there is no such thing.

Medicine links disease with death, health with life. Gaubius of Leyden (1705–80) gave this definition: "Medicine is the guardian of life and health against death and disease"; while today medicine says that evidence for the idea of a 'natural death' is wanting, because autopsies show that all death can be traced to the residues of disease. This implies the hope that could we do away with disease we might also do away with death. However, a diseased life and a healthy death are also realities. This rearrangement of the usual pairs offers another way of viewing death problems which the analyst meets. The battle against disease can be separated from dread of death, because disease is an enemy of both life and death. Disease interferes with proper dying as well as proper living. A Hindu metaphor of dying shows that *death requires health*; one drops intact and ripened from the tree of life at the right moment. This implies that the physician may take arms against disease not for the sake of life only but also *in the name of death*, in order to allow his charge to come to conscious fruition.

Or, for the Eskimos, when one falls ill, one takes on a

new name, a new diseased personality. To get over a disease, one must quite literally 'get over' it by transcending it, that is, by dying. The only hope for cure lies in the death of the ill personality. Health requires death.

Perhaps this is what Socrates meant with his last obscure words about owing a sacrificial cock to Asklepios. Once the cocky pride of life that crows hopefully at each day's dawning is sacrificed, the instinct for tomorrow is yielded. Death then is the cure and the salvation and not just a last, worst stage of a disease. The cock-crow at dawn also heralds resurrection of the light. But the victory over disease and the new day begins only when the ambition for it has been abandoned upon the altar. The disease which the experience of death cures is the rage to live.

This disease is phrased best in the medical-statistical term 'life-expectancy'. Hoping, 'expecting with desire', is justified statistically; one has the right to a certain quantity of life. This hope tends to entangle physician and patient in hoping for the wrong thing. They hope for more of the life that is already known, that is, for the past. Hope of this kind is hardly for salvation or even for new beginnings. It is regressive because it prevents the challenge of death. It is egotistic because it asks for more of what one was. This is hardly the hope Paul describes which is not seen and where 'getting better' would mean a quality of being, not an approach to the normal. One is led to believe that the desire to be free from illness means in truth to return to what one was before the illness, to the *status quo ante*. When the physician joins the patient in hoping to *re*store or *re*turn him to health with a speedy *re*covery, they move against the flow of time, the process of ageing, and the reality of death. Their joint hope denies the morbidity of all life.

An analyst often finds himself purposely passing by the symptoms appearing in his practice. Rather than investigate these symptoms, he turns to the person's life which has fostered the pathology. His premise is that the disease has its meaning in the life of the patient and he tries to understand this meaning. He cannot hold out the usual hope for cure or even relief of symptoms. His analytical experience says that *the hope which the patient presents is part of the pathology itself.* The patient's hope arises as an essential part of the constellation of his suffering. It is frequently governed by impossible demands to be free of suffering itself. The same condition that constellated the symptoms is just the condition which these symptoms are interrupting and killing—or curing. Therefore, an analyst does not hope for a return to that condition out of which the symptoms and the hope for relief arose.

Because hope has this core of illusion it favours repression. By hoping for the *status quo ante*, we repress the present state of weakness and suffering and all it can bring. Postures of strength are responsible for many major complaints today—ulcers, vascular and coronary conditions, high blood-pressure, stress syndrome, alcoholism, highway and sport accidents, mental breakdown. The will to fall ill, like the suicide impulse, leads patient and physician face to face with morbidity, which stubbornly returns in spite of all hope to the contrary. One might ask if medical hope itself is not partly responsible for recurrent illness; since it never fully allows for weakness and suffering the death experience is not able to produce its meaning. Experiences are cheated of their thorough effect by speedy recovery. *Until the soul has got what it wants, it must fall ill again.* And another iatrogenic vicious circle of recurrent illness begins.

The medical image of health, with its expectations upon life, simply does not allow enough for suffering. Medicine would rid us of it. The physician may aim to rid his patient of his disease because he views it as a foreign invasion to be thrown off. But 'getting rid' is impossible in analysis because, as we have seen, the disease is the patient. And the disease is the suffering not from which the patient must be saved but the condition necessary for salvation. If the patient is the disease, 'getting rid' means a destructive rejection of the patient. The patient's only protection here may be a magnified transference where the soul—cajoling, clinging, seducing—demands more intensely than ever to be allowed to be. As long as cure means 'getting rid', no person in analysis will ever want to give up being a patient.

Yet, it would seem the hope of medical treatment is to achieve that utopia where there are no patients. Somewhere, somehow, the patient always feels he 'ought not' to be ill. We are led by medicine itself, through its notion of health, to live beyond ourselves, driven and exhausted, in threat of breakdown, owing to the denial of human frailty. When the physician cautions to slow down, his own 'go, go, go' and *furor agendi* prevent his warning from having effect. 'Getting better' means 'getting stronger'; health has become equivalent to strength, strength to life. We are built up to break down and then be rebuilt as we were before, like a machine caught in an accelerated feedback. The soul seems able to make itself heard only by speaking the physician's language—symptoms.

To be weak and without hope, to be passive to the symptomatic manifestations of the unconscious, is often a highly positive condition at the beginning of analysis. It does not feel positive because our hope is for something else, for something we expect from what we have already known. But death is going on and a transformation is probable. An analyst may encourage his patient to experience these events, to welcome them, even to treasure them—for some get better by getting worse. If he starts to hope with the patient to 'get rid of' them he has begun to repress in a medical way. Some must arrive at this place where humility begins only through the humiliating defeat of disease or suicide attempts, only through the organic mode. But here medical hope with its armoury of prescriptions aims for the strength of the *status quo ante*. It sends the patient, strengthened, away again. As these patients were on their way to health by approaching death, medicine sends them back again to life and disease.

An analyst approaches dependence and passivity and hopelessness differently, because he starts from his own weakness. He is faced with admitting in the first hour that he can make no diagnosis, does not know the cause of the complaint, nor whether he can treat it or cure it. He shows that he is, in a sense, passive to it. He has had to abandon his expectations about the lives of his patients, and he offers little to feed a patient's hope. If he has hope at all, it is in the unconscious, in the unknown which might emerge out of the analytical dialectic, which is a hope "for that we see not". This attitude was presented in detail in the chapter "Meeting the Suicide Risk".

As with hoping, so it is with growing. The physician has been trained in biology. His model of development comes from studies of evolution, mainly on sub-human species. He recognises development by growth in size, differentiation in function, increased viability, approximation to the norm for the species, and in higher forms of life, he recognises ripeness by the capacity to reproduce. Genetics, bio-chemistry, histology, embryology have given the physician his basic knowledge about growth.

Transferred to the analytical process of soul development, this model misapprehends some fundamental phenomena. Here again we find Freudian analysis influenced by its medical background. Freudian analysis generally comes to an end when the patient has achieved successful sexual adjustment. Freudian analysis rarely accepts analysands over the age of forty-five. The notion of development is conditioned by biological thinking. The biological ability to reproduce is transferred to the psyche and made a criterion for 'maturity'. But must biological plasticity and psychic capacity coincide?

Even the idea of creativity, the cherished goal of so many people, is moulded by these biological notions of potency and reproduction. Because the seed of all natural processes always shows itself physically, creativity is conceived as a reproductive act with a tangible result—a child, a book, a monument—that has a physical life going beyond the life of its producer. Creativity, however, can be intangible in the form of a good life, or a beautiful act, or in other virtues of the soul such as freedom and openness, style and tact, humour, kindness. The ability to create virtue in oneself has always been for philosophy and religion a prime good. Traditionally, this kind of growth took precedence over physical growth. To achieve it, the biological model of creativity and the kind of growth shown by nature may have to be sacrificed. But growth in soul does not require the exaggerations of the martyr and ascetic. We need only recall that the creative life shows spontaneity and freedom, and that *creativity does not mean only productivity* of a voluminous physical sort. The patient wants to 'grow' and 'become creative'. And a good bit of psychotherapy is deluded by the idea that everyone must be normal (cured), having children, and 'doing things', or be creative by writing or painting or 'making things'. When a person talks about creativity as productivity he tends to find a receptive ear in the medical analyst because of the biological model of growth. (The medical attitude is correctly bound to this way of thinking because, as we recall, the root of 'physician' is *bhu*, meaning 'to grow', 'to produce'.)

This notion of growth betrays the same expectations as hoping. Again, it is quantitative. It tends to see the analytical process mainly as *adding to personality*. An analyst who so views things hopes his patient will grow more well rounded, more adapted, more successful, more productive. Or, if his goals be introverted, growth tends to mean a richer, more differentiated subjectivity, formulated as 'enlargement of consciousness'. Whether the expansion be extraverted or introverted, growth tends to mean increase and the goals are influenced by biological thinking. The person expects to grow along the lines of the biological model, and the analyst who stands altogether upon this model runs the risk of judging growth only according to the standards of evolutionary processes. Such ideas of development are more suitable for the growing child than for the grown adult, for whom increase of size and viability, reproduction, and approximation to the norm are no longer goals. Growth as increase only, growth without death, echoes the wish for a loving Mother with everflowing milk from her breast. Creativity as expansive productivity has in it the omnipotent fantasies of ambitious phallicism. Maintaining such goals into later life, even if now transferred on to 'psychic development' and 'creativity' reveals that not all childish things have been put away. It is the immature who are preoccupied with the search for maturity. And is it not typical of adolescence to see growth and creativity in protean images of 'becoming'? Hope and growth, like youth, are green. The creative *furor agendi*, supported by misplaced metaphors of growth, may prevent true psychic development, and so an analyst is led to view growth in a wholly other light.

The creativity of analysis does not have to go beyond the analysis itself. It does not have to produce something else. The creativity is there, present during the hour of analysis itself. The analytical relationship, that is, a relationship mutually worked at, is the basic form of mutual creativity. Other creative acts take place in solitude, as painting and writing, or in complex groups, as in the performing arts. But in analysis at its best two people create each other. Does not analysis provide the root metaphor for creativity in any relationship, where the fruitful interplay is the work but the work is not for its fruits?

The analytical process consists of transformations towards individuality; it leads to being oneself. From the empirical observation of this process one could state that individuality is the norm for the species, man. This is paradoxical, because individuality is always different from the species and belies all statistical truths. *The analyst therefore finds himself encouraging a growth that, if anything, leads towards the non-standard and eccentric.* He finds himself taking stands, as the stand on suicide, which seem definitely opposed to the norms for the species as biologically conceived.

Growth of the soul may lead altogether away from adaptability and differentiation. For example, through analysis a young introverted wife, or a young man for whom feeling comes before thinking, may find themselves more withdrawn and less in command of the world about them. They have had first to be what they are rather than get along with a world that for them makes inauthentic demands. On a longer view, perhaps they are now more adapted, but the steps towards this adaptation appear totally different from the usual biological notion of growth. Even some extremes of the asylum, such as increased dependence and autistic withdrawal, an analyst can see as phenomena of growth. The soul can make developments without their coming to light, and its manifestations may appear contrary to the world, life, and the body. We must think again about the ancient idea of a healthy mind in a healthy body. When we speak of a full life we do not always mean a full soul too. Sometimes a full life can mean an 'inner emptiness', just as someone said to be a rich soul or a good person may never have lived one day of his life in good health from a medical point of view.

The biological goals of enlargement and differentiation may have to be forsaken in behalf of concentration. For some gifted young men the horizon and all its luminous possibilities shrinks. The development of consciousness requires perseverance and single-mindedness. Concentration upon oneself and one's fate develops a narrowness of vision and emotional intensity that nowhere fit the pattern of biological differentiation or the viability of a well-rounded man who has brought all his faculties into play.

Analysis is just not dynamic psychotherapy. The very word 'psychodynamics' betrays the hopeful, growing *weltanschauung*. Analysis often leads to conditions where the dynamics of change fall away, ending in stability. This stability the alchemists understood as the Stone; not known for its capacity to grow and become different, but simply the same. The simplicity of this condition is not pessimistic, but it weighs heavily on optimistic expectations.

Growth may be a development away from the world. The analytical process shows this by images of losing, of shedding, of dying. Just as much falls away as is added. When illusions are worked through, what remains is often smaller than what was hoped, because becoming oneself means being reduced to just what one is—that stone of common clay—just as loving oneself means accepting one's limited reality, which is, as well, one's uniqueness. Analytical development, especially in older people, seems to move away from what shows to what does not show. (Again, is it not the child who must show us everything?) Questions of manifest results become less and less compelling, even though the analytical work may become more and more urgent. Here, creativity is fully occupied with the creation of oneself. We have discussed this above in the language of tradition as the subtle body, or immortal diamond body, or building one's death. Such growth and creativity cannot be measured by biological standards; it corresponds more with the patterns of spiritual development in religion, mysticism, and philosophy.

Therefore the analytical process is described better as qualitative refinement than as quantitative growth. Alchemy presents, as Jung so carefully documented, the clearest picture of this kind of development. Ore (our common substance) is smelted to yield a precious metal; fluids (our vague emotional currents) are distilled for a drop of rare essence; solid masses (our amorphous accumulations) are reduced to their elements. Separation proceeds by discrimination and the dross is discarded. Or, through the fire and salt (of our hot and bitter experiences) superfluities are burned away and values given permanence. The too gross is made subtle, the too heavy volatilised, the too mercurial burdened with lead, and the too dry fertilised with rain. The yield of the harvest is always smaller than the standing grain. The analytical work tends to produce the smaller personality in the religious sense, where growth seems to proceed downward and inward, and backward towards ancestral spirits and germinating seeds from which we have sprung. As alchemy says, the analytical process is an *opus contra naturam*, a work against nature. The soul's ontogeny hardly recapitulates biological phylogeny, even if our intellects must use biological metaphors for descriptions. Therefore, psychic growth is paradoxically a growth against natural life, when natural life is conceived too naïvely. The growth of the soul would be through death, the major *opus contra naturam*. No, it is not growth, but rather as the Buddha said in his last words: "Decay is inherent in all component things. Work at your salvation with diligence."

As hope and growth are inadequate for conceiving the analytical process, so too their opposites, despair and death, are also unsatisfactory metaphors. Or, rather, as long as we discuss analysis as a process of improvement only, any model of refinement, transformation, growth, and development will do. But all such root metaphors mislead when they become shields against *direct experience*. And direct experience, the soul's only food, is the heart of analysis, because it generates consciousness. Refinement, transformation, growth, and development all require individual moments of direct experience which negate in shattering intensity the process of accumulated development.

Process can too easily be confused with progress, progress too easily mask the moment. A moment, any moment in fact, can be the moment of death, so that the whole process is always condensed into the now. It is not elsewhere nor in the future, but here and now, at any moment of emotionally intense consciousness.

We know little about consciousness. After all the ages man has been in this world, we are still unable to say very much about the central event of psychic life. We have reliable hypotheses about its physiological base and sensory connections. We also have good reason to believe that consciousness consumes energy, that it requires psychological tension or 'set', and that it is bound up with what is called 'reality'. Conversely, we use the word unconscious when there is distortion or incognisance of reality. From what evidence we have, it seems that *consciousness intensifies when reality is experienced most boldly.*

166

This assumption accords with the descriptions of most spiritual disciplines which develop consciousness through intensifying focus into a prism of attention. This attention is not merely intellectual. It is an attending, waiting, or listening to reality speaking, an image for which is the Buddha—his huge receptive ears, the whole side of his head opened up. Consciousness is vivified in analysis by bold confrontations with reality, the paradigm of which is facing together the reality of death by suicide. Getting to this place where all veils fall is expressed in countless metaphors for the development of consciousness, such as: wandering the blind alleys and detours of the labyrinth; the progress of the pilgrim through inflations, depressions, and resistant obstacles; peeling away, one by one, the external wrappings of the Kabbalistic onion, and so on. Whatever the metaphor, the aim is to get through to a direct experience of reality, things just as they are. Mystical consciousness, even the chemical 'instant visions' of Huxley, aims at this vivid penetration, so that the division between subjective awareness here and objective nature there disappears. Life and imagination join in moments of synchronicity.

The detours, the walls, and the veils are those systems that we have constructed to prevent direct contact. They are the growth that prevent growth, the crusts that shield sensitivity from immediate exposure. For *immediacy is the great taboo*, and experience has become vicarious. The soul's food is packaged. The person no longer feels he is inside his own life, but is outside somewhere looking on or putting it into words. He has become a character in a film, the author of his own memoirs, a piece of the family's imagination fulfilling hopes sprung from the despair of others. Mother lives life through her children and Father through his organisation. Contact through sexuality becomes compulsive when every other possibility of naked immediacy recedes. The soul would bare itself to another in its simple eloquence but only impels the body into adulterous folly. Most subtly, experience is mediated by psychology itself, its heroes, their images and their lives, its techniques and terms. The person becomes a case report, acting out concepts from the book in a process of self-analysis that fragments emotional spontaneity into bits of dust. Even all the worthwhile activities of leisure and social responsibility, the hobbies of the suburb, as well as the 'higher' pursuits such as religion, art, and the idyll of personal love *can prevent direct experience* so that life takes on that quality called 'phony' by the young, who, because they are still capable of immediacy, resist with violence the caging of their pristine vision in the ready-made traps of adult avoidances. For this reason we have called analysis a continuous breakdown and have related it to creativity. It must be iconoclastic. *It proceeds by breaking the vessels in which experience is trapped, even the vessel of analysis itself.*

Of all the vessels, the medical one is the most tempting for the analyst, especially since it contains so nicely the expectations of the patient. By watching for growth and hoping for the next hour, the unfinished business of this hour may be avoided. In analysis there is only the numinous now; and growth and hope lead away from this confrontation. Here, only boldness will do, even to the point where therapeutic skill in the medical sense gives way to human directness and the risk of emotion. Here, we are naked and rather hopelessly dumb and in no way the patient's superior.

The analyst's only instrument for intensifying awareness during the analytical hour is his own person. Therefore, analysts have always considered their own analysis the primary criterion for the work; the unanalysed are lay. Dreams, associations, events may all come to his aid, but they may just as easily be used by the patient as new veils and new defences against direct experience. This makes the present encounter so important because in it the analyst not only mirrors the patient. He confronts him with the analyst's own reaction. The patient has come for this reaction. He seeks neither growth, nor love, nor cure, but consciousness in immediate reality. The present encounter requires the partners to be intensely focused, or 'all there', a kind of total 'being present', which owing to the physical basis of consciousness cannot be maintained at length. Again, as we discussed in Chapter VI, this total commitment to being in the process is the ontological ground of the work, because being analytically present means also the presence of analytical being.

The movement from couch to chair, that is, the movement from Freud to Jung, shows this shift away from the diagnostic and the mediate to the dialectical and the immediate. The physical position parallels another ontological position, giving another meaning to 'being in analysis'. The patient in the chair no longer looks down upon himself with the medical eye as an object for diagnosis and treatment. The change from couch to chair represents a shift in focus in the person himself from *what-he-has* to *who-he-is*. The armchair corners us into ourself, back into the inside of our reality, just as we are, face to face, knee to knee, boldly confronted in the mirror of the other, with not a chance for vicarious experience. There is no longer the freedom of association with the hopes for something new to turn up. There are no expectations for something different; instead there is the sameness of what one is, now. We experience the changeless beneath the recurrent changes. That sameness and changelessness the early Greeks called Being, and it is the sameness of one's uniqueness, which the Alchemists imaged in the Stone. Here, at this still and wounding point, there is neither hope nor growth, nor any becoming, but only what is now, and *deo concedente*, pure and clear as crystal.

The process can be described as a series of unique and priceless moments of clarity, which is often imaged in the psyche as a necklace of precious stones. Tradition has referred to the construction of these prismatic moments as building the diamond body. The relevance of the analytical work for realising in the soul the indestructible values of consciousness to our theme of death, immortality, and building the diamond body now emerges.

Could we not then conclude that the patient who comes to solve his psychological problem is at bottom asking to solve the problem of his psyche; that is to say, to solve one's problem means to solve or save one's soul. This is what tradition has always called salvation or redemption. We find that behind all urges to grow and develop, to create and produce, to hope for more strength, for more life and more time, behind the go, go, go, is the need to save one's soul, one way or another, by hook or by crook, through hell and high water, by Zen or by Freud or by Jung. Through the direct experience made possible in analysis we do as the Buddha said: "Work at your salvation with diligence."

CHAPTER XII

MEDICAL SECRECY AND THE ANALYTICAL MYSTERY

LET us turn now to see whether the secrecy of analysis depends upon medical secrecy as set down first in the Oath of Hippocrates: "Whatever I see or hear, professionally or privately, which ought not to be divulged, I will keep secret and tell no one." If other than a medical ground can be shown for analytical secrecy, then we will have met still another argument against 'lay' analysis.

Medical secrecy is a noble ethical principle. It safeguards the dignity of the person and, at the same time, elevates disease itself by regarding it as belonging to a person's fate, part of his tragedy and something to respect. There is also a social necessity in medical secrecy. Where health and disease are conceived to reveal the ups and downs of fortune, it is imperative that the physician not gossip about the affairs of his charges. Without the ethics of medicine, medicine would hardly be possible. Who would let the physician in to see his weakest and most disgusting sides if the physician were to carry tales from the sickroom to the market place? However, for all its honour, medical secrecy may often be but a programmatic kind of secrecy.

It tends to be programmatic because it is a rule, and rules handle all cases alike. Medical secrecy tends to leave out of account the *individual relationship of patient and physician*, so that the patient is indeed 'in the physician's hands', or 'under the surgeon's knife'. The physician does not begin with identifying himself with the case before him. This is not modern medicine, for all the reasons we have been discussing. The physician needs his rule about medical secrecy *to protect the patient*, because he does not feel that the case affects him. He does not sense that medical secrecy aims also to protect the physician, in that presenting a case is also somewhere an exposure of himself. Were the physician involved emotionally like the analyst in the therapeutic process, there would not be the same need for a rule of secrecy. Then he would feel constrained to keep silent about his patient's soul as he does about his own. Discretion would not need to be imposed by rule because it would spring naturally.

A rule is imposed from without when the natural sense of discretion has been lost. In antiquity the Oath of Hippocrates had religious overtones which have been stripped away by modern medicine. What remains is but a rigid skeleton, an ethical principle without its transcendent vitality. The physician says: "You may tell me everything, show me everything, because by my oath it will go no further." But the physician says nothing about himself and how he receives these revelations of another person's soul. *A secret shared produces intimacy, and the first person the patient is concerned with is not 'others', but the physician himself.* Is he worthy of entering so deeply in my private life? Is the physician up to handling the revelations he demands? Yet the patient has been cornered by the rule into intimacy with a stranger.

Medical secrecy works through a curious dissociation. The patient presents his case history and his body as if both were outside his inner life. The physician examines the case history and the body of the patient as if they were objects. For the medical situation there probably could be no other way, and medical secrecy suffices. The body is anyway not concealed as is the soul; its facts are objectified, public, whereas the soul is in essence private and secret. Hence, when the old physicians sought the locus of the soul they looked in the most hidden recesses of the body, just as medically influenced analysts of today conceive psychic life intimately bound up with the 'privates', the 'secret parts'.

Wrong secrets and those kept wrongly cut one off and act like poison from within, so that confession is cathartic and communication therapeutic. The paranoid demand for absolute loyalty, that fear of betrayal and exposure, shows that one is no longer able to love and be hurt. Loving goes where betrayal is possible, otherwise there is no risk. Loving in safety is the smaller part of loving. Secrecy of this sort is a defence leading to paranoid loneliness: alone with one's secrets and no one to trust. Another secret kept wrongly is that of the small child who clutches his secret in powerful exercise of omnipotence. For him it is necessary, but the grown-up child goes on in this pattern, dominating by holding back. Both paranoid and childish secrecy keep one wrongly apart.

To keep a secret means etymologically to keep something apart, separate. Secrecy is basic for individuality. In a family, for instance, no individual personalities can develop unless the members keep some secrets *with* one another and other secrets *from* one another. What you keep secret keeps you apart, and in your secret life you begin to discover your individual soul. (One reason why it is so difficult to keep secrets is just because it is so hard to maintain one's individuality.)

By telling a secret one lets another into the sacred preserve of one's individuality. One keeps one's secrets until one feels that the other person with whom one is about to share a secret also views it as sacred. For this, trust must be built up between two people. Trust comes about slowly through understanding and dialectic. *A secret can be shared only between two people, not between one person and a profession.* When the analyst withholds his personality in accordance with medical secrecy, hoping to create an atmosphere where he is but an objective reflector of events, he may actually be preventing revelations which the patient needs, not just to release, but desperately to share with another human being. We open not only to let *out* a secret, but to let someone else *in* on the secret. The analytical point of view tends to regard secrets as something to be shared, like a communal meal. Because participation in a secret builds relationship, a patient's reluctance to reveal himself, or even let himself be tested psychologically, can be a good beginning for the analytical work. It shows how highly he values his private life, his soul history. But secrecy prevents accurate diagnosis; and secrecy refuses the Apollonic urge to bring everything to light. So the medical point of view tends to regard all secrets as wrong secrets. They are something to be got out of the patient's system by abreaction and catharsis. They must be told freely, whatever pops into the mind, to make a clean breast. Thus Freudian analysis was originally called the 'talking cure'.

Analysis, as we have been conceiving it from the first Chapter, is a secret league. Its trust develops through secrecy. If it is ethically wrong for the analyst to break this trust by discussing the analysand, then it is also a breach of the secret league for the analysand to report on his analysis and his analyst. The secret kept by the two with each other may not be opened *by either* without being broken. To break a secret is to break a promise, which means nothing else than breaking the promise of an analysis. This promise is not hope for some specific result, although it has the suggestion of pregnancy. The secret the partners keep gives promise for things to come. Containing a secret is thus the first action in building the analytical container which holds the analytical promise.

This idea is imaged by the "analytical vessel" documented by Jung in his alchemy studies. The loyalty of the two to each other in their common work is an indispensable demand of the work itself. Without the secret league, we cannot meet the suicide risk. This secrecy is more than a rule imposed by ethics. It has quite other grounds which are closer to those of the religious mysteries.

The word mystery comes from the Greek *myein*, which is used both for the closing of the petals of a flower as well as of the eyelids. It is a natural movement of concealment, showing the piety of shame before the mystery of life, half of which takes place in the dark. Analysts who retain an only sexual view of the transference may tend to overlook that shame, concealment, and mystery may be virtues. Some processes must be kept secret if they are to function at all. For example, secrecy is appropriate to creative activities, to the relationship of lovers, to prayer, contemplation, and retreat. The extraordinary thing about our major experiences is that they are so secretly intimate, meaning just us, personally, individually. All that is dark is not necessarily repressed. And what is deep in depth psychology—even if conceived on a biological model as rooted down in the dirt and darkness—must remain underground. The source is out of sight.

Analysis is cautious about unravelling repressions. Since the repressed anyway returns in one form or another, digging, with the spirit of *furor agendi*, may be premature and damage the whole plant. Therefore, when investigating repressed sexuality, let us not go too far and expose what it is natural to conceal. The numinous is guarded by taboo and the genitals are usually covered in most societies. Frank discussion of sexuality can violate the feelings of secrecy that are natural to sexual life. Intercourse is not usually a public event, and the moments of reproduction, from the descent of the ovum and the production of sperm to fertilisation and gestation, all take place in the dark. This means that when bringing sexual secrets and guilt to light, let us leave sexual mystery and shame in the dark.

Of the analogies with the analytical mystery, the religious mystery perhaps serves best. Where secrecy keeps silent about the known, mystery concerns the unknown and the unknowable. The participant in a religious mystery shares an experience which he does not bring about himself. He is witness to an epiphany of a God, a drama which draws his soul into its events, and through this experience he is transformed. His witness is not that of the detached observer, nor is his emotional participation that of the enthusiast. He takes part by being open to what may come, allowing himself to be moved by something transcending his own will. In Greece those who took part in the greater mysteries—and there could be thousands present at a time—never told what took place, and to this day we do not 'know', in the scientific sense, precisely the content and sequences of these mysteries. They did not tell for fear of death, because a mystery in which one participates creates not just secrecy, not just discretion, but an overpowering silent awe which makes impossible telling someone who did not share the same experience. *The participators themselves do not 'know'.* Religious life depends on such experiences, and a house of God springs up wherever a mystery has occurred. Cults form naturally out of the analytical mystery.

One cannot report about a mystery, because one cannot speak about what one is in. 'About' means 'from the outside', and to get there where report is possible one would have to leave where one is. The participant in a mystery is still in as long as the vessel is closed. To step out of a living experience by telling about it means to share no longer this livingness. It means death.

If we agree that the analytical relationship is a secret league and that the analytical process is a mystery, then some of the secretiveness of transference is seen to be not only subterfuge and resistance but also a legitimate aspect of the process. The analysand is not a medical patient trying to keep back bits of his case history. He is obliged to withhold his soul until he feels that the bond between him and the analyst is not a programmatic condition imposed by the rule of a profession, but is a real connection. Or, later, when an analysis moves towards separation, this phase can be indicated by keeping back secrets. The other person begins to withhold his soul, feeding his own individuality with his own unshared experiences.

This leads to these observations: firstly, resistance, secretiveness, silence, and suspicion slow the process down. These hindrances prove so difficult to meet that one must ask why they appear at all, if not precisely to make the transformations more solid and lasting. Secrecy thus cements not only the bonds between the two partners but also the integration going on within the psyche of the analysand. When an analysand blocks at free association we have an indication of a resisting complex. But complexes, as we have seen, cannot be reduced by force and their resistance overcome. Their core is always a feeling-toned idea, an unassailable experience, that has to be secret because it is a fundamentally unknown and numinous mystery. This core cannot be known until its archetypal meaning comes out in experiences—and this may take as long as life. *Resistance and secrecy therefore are based upon the unknown and unknowable at the core of psychic life.*

Secondly, analysts are justified in their stubborn refusal to present in a paper every detail of an analysis. Some

177

things may never be told, not even when a person has died, since secrets belong to a soul, and whether the soul has died too we do not know. Moreover, some things may never be told because they can never be told; they do not admit formulation. Formulation turns the unknown at the core of psychic life into a 'problem'. And it is an error to confuse psychological problems with the mysteries of the soul, on the one hand mystifying problems, while on the other trying to resolve mysteries. The soul, though problematic, is not a problem, but a mystery. The analyst, though a problem-solver, is as well a *myste*, the initiated one who keeps the secret. *Problems can be solved; mysteries only lived.*

Lastly, the resistance the analyst feels to explanations of human behaviour is firmly based. His feelings do not arise from romantic cloudiness and a taste for obfuscations. To the contrary, the analyst serves Apollo, and he works day and night to clarify and illuminate. He is forced to think hard and speak concisely. However, analysis teaches its practitioners how much of human life is concealed in unconsciousness. By accepting this darkness, he can work within it. If the soul is a mystery, explanations will always fall short.

The mystery of the therapeutic process is the true background of analytical secrecy. It is altogether different from medical secrecy, which means that the medical degree, oath, and code are not needed to guarantee the closed vessel. The closed vessel is the receptacle for the transcendent, impersonal forces of the psyche which produce the healing. This healing is prepared behind the curtain in the wings. Some have experienced these impersonal forces as Gods, whose performance in the healing process makes it a drama reflected in dreams. Each dream has its dramatic structure, and the series of dreams unfolds the plots, the scenic inscapes, and the characters of the soul

178

history. This therapeutic drama is one long mythological epic in which the Gods and the patient and the analyst take part. When the Gods come on stage all falls silent and the eyelids close. Dipped into oblivion by this experience, one emerges without knowing precisely what has happened; one knows only that one has been changed.

Glencullen House, Co. Dublin/
Botorp, Hemsö,
1962–64.

REFERENCES—PART I

Achille-Delmas, F. *Psychologie pathologique du suicide*. Paris, 1932.

Alexander, I. E., and Adlestein, A. M. 'The psychology of death: three recent studies'. *Internat. J. Parapsy.*, III, 2, 1961.

Augustine. *The City of God*, I, 19.

Bartel, R. 'Suicide in eighteenth-century England: the myth of a reputation'. *Huntington Library Quarterly*, XXIII, 2, 1960.

Benz, E. 'Das Todesproblem in der stoischen Philosophie'. *Tübinger Beiträge zur Altertumswissenschaft*. Stuttgart, 1929.

Bettelheim, B. *The Informed Heart*. Glencoe, Ill., 1960.

Blackstone, W. 'Public wrongs'. *Commentaries on the Laws of England*, IV. 15th ed. London, 1809.

Bridgman, P. W. *The Intelligent Individual and Society*. New York, 1938.

Brown, N. O. *Life Against Death*. New York, 1959.

Camus, A. *The Myth of Sisyphus*. London, 1955.

Crocker, L. G. 'Discussion of suicide in the eighteenth century'. *J. Hist. Ideas*, XIII, 1, 1952.

Curtis, H. J. 'Biological mechanisms underlying the aging process'. *Science*, 141, 3582, 1963.

Des Étangs, A. *Du suicide politique en France depuis 1789 jusqu'a nos jours*. Paris, 1860.

Durkheim, E. *Suicide*. London, 1952.

Eissler, K. R. *The Psychiatrist and The Dying Patient*. New York, 1955.

Epidemiological and Vital Statistics Report, 14, 5. World Health Organization. Geneva, 1961.

Farberow, N. L., and Shneidman, E. S. (eds.). *The Cry For Help*. New York, 1961.

Fedden, R. *Suicide*. London, 1938.

Federn, Meng, Sadger, Lorand, *et al*. 'Selbstmord'. *Zschft. f. psychoanal. Pädagogik*, III, 11/12/13, 1929.

Feifel, H. (ed.). *The Meaning of Death*. New York, 1959.

Frederiksen, Sv. 'The soul and healing in Eskimo Shamanism'. (Lectures given at the C. G. Jung Institute, Zurich, 1963.)

Freud, S. *Beyond the Pleasure Principle*. London, 1950.

—— 'Thoughts for the times on war and death'. *Collected Papers*, IV. London, 1949.

Gordon, R. 'The death instinct and its relation to the Self'. *J. Analyt. Psychol.*, 6, 1961.

Heidegger, M. *Sein und Zeit*, I. Halle, 1927.

Herzog, E. *Psyche und Tod*. Zurich, 1960.

Heywood and Massey. *Court of Protection Practice*. London, 1961.

Hume, D. 'On suicide'. *The Philosophical Works of David Hume*, IV. Boston and Edinburgh, 1854.

Jackson, D. D. 'Suicide'. *Scientif. Amer.*, November 1954.

Jacobsohn, H. 'Das Gespräch eines Lebensmuden mit seinem Ba'. *Zeitlose Dokumente der Seele*. Zurich, 1952.

Jankélévitch, V. 'La pensée de la mort et la mort de l'être pensant'. *Filosofia della Alienazione e Analisi Esistenziale*, ed. E. Castelli. Padova, 1961.

Jung, C. G. 'Concerning rebirth'. *The Archetypes and the Collective Unconscious* (*Collected Works* 9, 1). London and New York, 1959.

—— 'The soul and death'. *The Structure and Dynamics of the Psyche* (*Collected Works* 8). London and New York, 1960.

—— 'The psychology of the unconscious'. *Two Essays on Analytical Psychology* (*Collected Works* 7). London and New York, 1953.

Klopfer, B. 'Suicide: the Jungian point of view'. *The Cry for Help*, ed. Farberow and Shneidman, *q.v.*

Lawrence, D. H. *The Complete Poems*. London, 1957.

Le Moal, P. *Suicide, chantage du suicide, chez l'enfant et l'adolescent*. Paris, 1944.

Leopold, A. C. 'Senescence in plant development'. *Science*, 134, 1727, 1961.

Meerloo, J. A. M. *Suicide and Mass Suicide*. New York, 1962.

Menninger, K. *Man Against Himself*. New York, 1938.

Morgenthaler, W. 'Letzte Aufzeichnungen von Selbstmördern'. *Beiheft z. Schweiz. Zschft. f. Psychol. u. i. Anwend.*, 1. Bern, 1945.

Natanson, M. 'Death and situation'. *Amer. Imago*, 16, 4, 1959.

Osis, K. 'Deathbed observations by physicians and nurses'. *Parapsy. Monographs*, 3. New York, 1961.

Osler, W. 'To the editor of the *Spectator*'. Oxford, 4 November 1911. See Feifel, p. 248.

Plato. *Phaedo*.

Plessner, H. 'On the relation of time to death'. *Man and Time: Papers from the Eranos Yearbooks*, 3. London and New York, 1958.

Ringel, E. *Der Selbstmord*. Wien and Dusseldorf, 1953.

—— *Neue Untersuchungen zum Selbstmordproblem*. Wien, 1961.

Sartre, J.–P. *L' Être et le néant*. Paris, 1943.

Shneidman, E. S. 'Orientations towards death'. *The Study of Lives*, ed. R. W. White. New York, 1963.

——, and Farberow, N. L. 'Suicide and death'. In Feifel, *q.v.*

Spinoza. *Ethica*, IV.

Sprott, S. E. *The English Debate on Suicide from Donne to Hume*. La Salle, Ill., 1961.

de Stael (Baroness of Holstein). *Reflections on Suicide*. London, 1813.

Stengel, E., Cook, N., and Kreeger, I. S. *Attempted Suicide*. London, 1958.

Sym, J. *Life's Preservative against Selfkilling or an Useful treatise concerning Life and Self-murder* . . . London, 1637.

Turner, J. W. C. *Kenny's Outlines of Criminal Law*. Cambridge, 1952.

——, ed. *Russell on Crime*. London, 1958.

Webb, W. B. 'An overview of sleep as an experimental variable (1940–1959)'. *Science*, 134, 1421–23, 1961.

Wesley, J. 'Thoughts on suicide'. *Works*, XV. London, 1812.

Williams, M. 'The fear of death'. *J. Analyt. Psychol.*, (Part I) 3, 1958; (Part II) 7, 1962.

Willoughby, C. A., and Chamberlain, J. *MacArthur 1941–1951—Victory in the Pacific*. London, 1958.

REFERENCES—PART II

Burnet, Macfarlane. *Natural History of Infectious Disease.* 3rd ed. Cambridge, 1962.

Christou, E. *The Logos of the Soul.* (Dunquin Press, Blackwells, Oxford), Vienna/Zurich, 1963.

Clark-Kennedy, A. E. *Human Disease.* London, 1957.

Dubos, R. *Mirage of Health.* London, 1960.

Ekstein, R., and Wallerstein, R. S. *The Teaching and Learning of Psychotherapy.* New York, 1958.

Eliot, T. S. *Four Quartets.* London, 1944.

Entralgo, P. Lain. 'Menschliche Gesundheit und menschliche Vollkommenheit'. *Antaios,* IV, 5, 1963.

—— *Mind and Body.* London, 1955.

Freud, S. 'Papers on technique'. *Collected Papers,* II. London, 1953.

—— *The Question of Lay Analysis.* London (Imago), 1947.

Freud, Sachs, Jones, Horney, Nunberg, Reich, Alexander, *et al.* 'Diskussion der "Laienanalyse"'. *Internat. Ztschrft. f. Psychoanal.,* XIII, 1, 2, 3, 1927.

Hillman, J. *Emotion: A Comprehensive Phenomenology of Theories and Their Meanings for Therapy.* London, 1960.

—— 'Training and the C. G. Jung Institute, Zurich'. *J. Analyt. Psychol.,* 7, 1962.

Jones, E. *Sigmund Freud: Life and Work,* III. London, 1957.

Jung, C. G. *The Practice of Psychotherapy* (*Collected Works,* 16). London and New York, 1954.

—— *Psychology and Alchemy.* (*Collected Works,* 12). New York and London, 1953.

——, with A. Jaffé. *Memories, Dreams, Reflections.* New York and London, 1963.

Kerenyi, K. *Der Göttliche Arzt.* Darmstadt (Gentner), 1956.

Lewin, B. D., and Ross, H. *Psychoanalytic Education in the United States.* New York, 1960.

Martí-Ibáñez, F. *Centaur: Essays on the History of Medical Ideas.* New York, 1958.

Mayer, C. F. 'Metaphysical trends in modern pathology'. *Bull. Hist. Med.* 1952.

Meier, C. A. *Antike Inkubation und Moderne Psychotherapie.* Zurich, 1949.

Meier, C.A. 'Gedanken uber ärtzliche und nichtärtzliche Psychotherapie'. *Rev. Suisse de Psychol.*, 4, 1946.

Meillet, A. *Dictionnaire Etymologique de la Langue Latine*. Paris, 1951.

Menninger, K. *Love Against Hate*. New York, 1942.

Olmsted, J. M. D., and Olmsted, E. H. *Claude Bernard and the Experimental Method in Medicine*. New York, 1952 (1961).

Panofsky, D. and E. *Pandora's Box*. Bollingen Series. New York, 1956.

Prince, G. S. 'Medical psychology?'. *Brit J. Med. Psychol.*, 36, 299, 1963.

Robbins, S. L. *Textbook of Pathology*. Philadelphia, 1957.

Roblin, M. 'Le nom du médicin dans les langues d'Europe et les origines de la médicine'. *Médicine de France*, 122, 1961.

Sarasin, P. 'Zur Frage der Laienanalyse'. *Schweiz. Zschft. f. Psychol. u. i. Anwend.*, XV, 1, 1956.

Severinghaus, A. E., *et al. Preparation for Medical Education in the Liberal Arts Colleges*. New York and London, 1953.

Simon, H. J. *Attenuated Infection*. Philadelphia, 1960.

Skeat, W. W. *Etymological Dictionary of the English Language*. 4th ed. 1910.

Walde, A. *Vergleichendes Wörterbuch der Indogermanischen Sprachen*. Berlin and Leipzig, 1930.

Wartman, W. B. *Medical Teaching in Western Civilization*. Chicago, 1961.

Zimmer, H. *The King and the Corpse*. Bollingen Series. New York, 1948.

—— *Myths and Symbols in Indian Art and Civilization*. Bollingen Series. New York, 1946.

INDEX

Law; church, 27; continental law, 29; English, 27; Roman, 27

Lawrence, D. H., 11, 14, 96

Lay analysis, vii, 97, 101, 103, 104, 106, 109, 110–11, 118, 139, 171; analyst, 18–19, 21–2, 55, 82, 100, 105, 110–11, 112, 145, 168; physician, 86

Legal view of suicide, 27–30

Leopold, 58

Life: after death, 57, 66; and death, 59, 60, 61–2, 63–4, 68, 69, 106, 107, 152; and death experience, 91; expectancy, 157; expectancy curve, 35, 58; and hope, 154–5; outer, 77; processes, 58; promotion of, 34, 35, 36, 82, 129, 140, 155, 156; questions, 149; truth of, 86

Love, lovers, loving, 16, 19, 38, 46, 59, 64, 65, 77, 80, 85, 90, 101, 113, 116, 164, 168, 173, 175

Masturbation, 65

Mayer, Robert, 67

Meaning, 41, 112, 148–9

Medical; aims, 33–4; analysis, 22, 109, 123, 126, 143; attitude, 116–17; practitioner, 114; thinking, mode of, 105, 112, 139; treatment, 34, 83–4, 85–6; view, 104, 105; words, 113–18

Medicine, 100, 101, 102, 114, 115, 116; and analysis, 102, 104, 105, 106, 108, 111, 115, 139; and Apollo, 122, 123; Asklepian, 102, 122; and death, 119, 156; and diagnosis, 140–1; and health, 158, 159; Hippocratic, 102; and life, 155, 156; older approach of, 118; and pathology, 129, 134–5; psychological background of, 102; and psychology,

138; schools of, 120; and the soul, 102, 112–13

Meier, 122

Melancholy, 70

Memories, Dreams, Reflections, 151

Menninger, 59

Morbid, the, 134; states, 127

Morgenthaler, 69

Mother, 119, 124, 129, 162, 167

Myth, 78, 147, 151, 152

Mythic; fragments, 99; pattern, 80–1, 99

Mystery, 175, 176, 178

Mythology, inner, 51, 52, 78

Nietzsche, 64, 112

Nervous breakdown, 68, 168

Neurosis, 23, 43, 68, 82, 100

Norm, normal, 134–5, 163

Ontology, 68, 114; of analysis, 97, 98, 99, 107, 169; existential 99; of psychology, 100, 101

Osis, 69

Osler, 69

Pain, 131, 132, 133

Pandora, 154

Paradox, 46, 69, 79, 91, 107, 148, 163

Pathological bias, 128–9, 130, 131, 132, 133, 134, 135, 137, 138

Pathology, 117, 118, 127, 130, 131, 135, 147, 158; sexual, 135; statistical, 134–5

Personality, 78, 132, 162; disorders, 104

Philosophy, 58–63, 133

Physical; behaviour, 34; changes, 71; death, 69, 83, 84, 88; health, 34; life, 20, 21, 23, 66, 69, 74; medicine, 121; reality, 85, 107; treatment, 131

Thresholds, Crises and Transformations

Anima as Fate   Cornelia Brunner

The first translation into English of a 1963 work by a respected Swiss
analyst and longtime associate of C. G. Jung, who contributed the preface.
The first part explores the notion of the anima, the contrasexual aspect of
a man's psyche, in the works of Rider Haggard, particularly in his novel
She. The book's second part traces the development of the anima in a
series of dreams that a middleaged physician experienced while in analysis
over a period of several years. (xv, 277 pp.)

The Dream of Poliphilo   Linda Fierz-David

Back in print after some thirty years, this early Bollingen Series volume
was written by a close collaborator of Jung's who was a founding lecturer
at the Jung Institute, Zurich. Fierz-David interprets the *Hypnerotomachia*,
published during the Italian Renaissance, which recounts the dream of
Poliphilo as he is led by his beloved through a series of fantastic adven-
tures in a legendary landscape. Polia, who speaks for the sensate spirit of
the Renaissance, frees Poliphilo from his introverted obsession with
alchemy and the medieval restrictions of courtly love. Led back into clas-
sical culture, he awakens transformed by the love of his guide and deep-
ened into the archetypal background of love and sexuality that ancient
humanism provides. Foreword by C. G. Jung. Illustrations. (iii, 245 pp.)

In MidLife: A Jungian Perspective   Murray Stein

Midlife stirs fears of change and loss, so that as we approach this crucial
life passage we brace for a crisis. Drawing on myths—especially of
Hermes—and analytic practice, the author notes three important elements
in every passage: first a loss of energy and desire; followed by a new spirit,
renegade and mischievous, for whom established norms hold no attraction; finally comes a gift, a deep change in the personality. (149 pp.)

Hermes: Guide of Souls   Karl Kerényi

Karl Kerényi, mythographer, classicist and friend of Jung, here presents a
beautiful, authoritative study of the great God whom the Greeks revered
as Guide of Souls. Chapters on Hermes and Night, Hermes and Eros,
Hermes and the Goddesses illuminate the complex role of the God in clas-
sical mythology, while also providing an archetypal background for the
guiding of souls in psychotherapy, their passages between realms.
(104 pp.)

Spring Publications, Inc. • P.O. Box 222069 • Dallas, TX 75222